Expansion
& Innovation

The Story of Western Engineering
1954-1999

The Alexander Charles Spencer Engineering Building, 1959
(Ron Nelson Photography Ltd/File photo, Faculty of Engineering Science).

G. S. PETER CASTLE
and
GEORGE S. EMMERSON

ISBN: 978-1-4834-1502-4 (sc)
ISBN: 978-1-4834-1503-1 (e)

Because of the dynamic nature of the Internet, any web addresses or links contained in this book may have changed since publication and may no longer be valid. The views expressed in this work are solely those of the author and do not necessarily reflect the views of the publisher, and the publisher hereby disclaims any responsibility for them.

Any people depicted in stock imagery provided by Thinkstock are models, and such images are being used for illustrative purposes only. Certain stock imagery © Thinkstock.

Lulu Publishing Services rev. date: 8/26/2014

To Judy, my dear wife and best friend, who has shared 56 of the 57 years of my involvement with Western Engineering.

G.S.P.C.

Who-so-ever, in writing modern history, shall follow truth too near the heels, it may haply strike out his teeth. – Sir Walter Rayleigh

G.S.E.

Acknowledgements

In writing a work of this sort that tries to summarize the outcomes and efforts of so many people over a 45-year period it was essential to retrieve as much accurate information as possible from a great many different sources. Everyone I approached has been wonderfully cooperative and I thank them very much.

It is impossible to properly acknowledge each individual who has aided in this task but following are some who have been particularly helpful and to each I express my sincere gratitude:

Former Dean Mohan Mathur, who provided enthusiastic encouragement and support throughout the project, supplied valuable data and carefully proofread the material in various iterations.

Dean Andrew Hrymak for suggesting and supporting this project along with all the staff of Western Engineering, particularly Lesley Mounteer, Nina Lowes, Susan Chapman, Virginia Daugharty, and Allison Stevenson. Each have offered enthusiastic help and encouragement and showed surprising patience when confronted by requests for information.

Alan Noon for all his help with photo research and providing copies of his own images, as well as those from Western Archives. He generously shared his knowledge and expertise by restoring some of the older, lower quality photos. In addition, he kindly offered his extensive knowledge of Western to verify facts and events.

Heather Hughes, who came into the project in the latter stages, who edited the text and shepherded the material through the various stages required for publication.

Tom Belton, Robin Keirstead, Barry Arnott and all the collections centre staff at Western Archives for their cooperation and help in locating various historical documents and photos.

Reem Tabbara, who as a second-year student, helped immensely in preparing material for the Appendices.

And finally a special thank you to all the members of faculty, staff and former students who have taken the time to share information and report personal anecdotes of their experiences in Western Engineering. It is through these stories and pictures the history is able to come alive and adds flavour and meaning to the events. Unfortunately, there was not room for everything to be included and hopefully many wonderful stories will remain preserved for the next author of Western Engineering's legacy.

G.S.P.C.

Contents

Foreword

When I was asked to write the foreword to *Expansion & Innovation: The Story of Western Engineering 1954-1999*, it was a great honour, but came as a total surprise.

Although I eventually made it to the Dean's List, my rather checkered academic record beforehand did not exactly make me the obvious choice for the honour of writing the foreword. Perhaps the length of time it took me to graduate uniquely qualified me; as by then, I had firsthand experience with Professor Lauchland and Deans Dillon, Chess and Johnson, a great majority of the professors and probably participated in more pranks than my more proficient classmates.

I later had the opportunity to work with Deans Mathur, Berruti and Hrymak assisting, along with fellow graduates, as an Advisory Council Chair, University Renaissance Campaign Co-Chair and eventually Western's Chancellor.

No one is more qualified to chronicle the history of Engineering at Western than Peter Castle. After graduating in 1961, he returned several years later to become the first student to be awarded a PhD from the Faculty of Engineering Science. He was then appointed to the faculty where he remained for a 36-year career, including a term as assistant dean and two terms as department chair.

He still advises graduate students from his office on campus in the Thompson Building and in doing so, has had a continual vantage point from which to write this history commemorating Engineering's 60-year history at Western.

In the book, Peter includes excerpts from Professor George Emmerson's memoirs of the early years. He traces the origins of Engineering at Western from its two-year pre-engineering program of 20 students in 1954 and through its various stages of expansion and innovation. The story concludes at the beginning of the

John M. Thompson
(File photo courtesy of Communications and Public Affairs, Western University)

third millennium with the increased research, industry partnerships and growth of the graduate school.

The most important strategic decisions, ground-breaking research and the leadership initiatives that led to the faculty's phenomenal development are encapsulated in the narrative and serve as a reminder to future leaders of the great things that can be accomplished.

The history is also peppered with delightful anecdotes and reminiscences supplied by former students and staff. A description of a fourth-year project to build a Solar Car to travel across Australia is one of the intriguing stories. Many pictures of the more famous engineering pranks serve to validate the often-told tales, still repeated by alumni to this day. Some have even finally disclosed their names!

Currently, the Faculty of Engineering at Western has become one of Canada's great engineering schools and now encompasses some 1,550 undergraduate students, 590 graduate students and 200 teaching and support staff.

All who are affiliated with Engineering at Western will find this history interesting, informative and entertaining and a most suitable work to commemorate the 60th anniversary.

Peter Castle has deliberately not recorded the history beyond the year 2000, as he rightfully points out that it takes the passage of some years for events to turn into history. However, he has provided the starting point and inspiration to continue the story as time rolls on. So, I encourage others to follow in his footsteps and continue the narrative in the future.

Happy 60th anniversary!

John M. Thompson, O.C., BESc'66, LLD'94, PEng
Chancellor Emeritus, Western University

Preface

This history has been written at the suggestion of Dean Andrew Hrymak to mark the 60th anniversary in September 2014 of the start of Engineering Science at Western. The careful reader will note that the title promises only the first 45 years, 1954-99. Why this discrepancy? There are two reasons. The first is simple: although yesterday qualifies as history, it takes time for events to pass before they can be put in perspective and related in context. The second reason is much more pragmatic: the chapters which follow are divided into eras under the headings of the leaders of the periods – a president, a department head, and four deans – all of whom are either deceased (Dr. G. Edward Hall and professors Stuart Lauchland, Richard Dillon, Ab Johnson and Gordon Chess), or retired (former Dean Mohan Mathur). The two subsequent Deans, Franco Berruti and Andrew Hrymak, are still very active in the faculty. As a result, it shall be left for a future faculty historian to document these years.

I gratefully acknowledge co-authorship of this work by my late colleague George S. Emmerson, in recognition of the fact he wrote a history of the first 25 years in 1979. At the time, this work was not widely circulated. In the present version, much of the text in the first few chapters is preserved as George wrote it, however I have taken the liberty of editing some details, and added photographs and reminiscences from faculty, staff and former students. I hope he would be content with the changes and additions made to his eloquent text, and he would still reaffirm his comment, "I salute with curiosity the future historians of the faculty."

I also acknowledge an immense debt of gratitude to my good friend, colleague and former Dean, Mohan Mathur. His period of deanship marked one of the most innovative periods in the history of Engineering Science at Western. It has been a great privilege for me to work with him during this exciting era. Although he has been retired from Western for several years, he still has strong ties with the faculty and has been of great help as I put this document together. He contributed information, advice and encouragement, as well as carefully reading it at various stages of editing.

The period of interest in this story, the 1950s to the 1990s, is one that is fascinating to contemplate in the perspective of modern history. In two generations, society has changed dramatically in ways that are too complex to try to summarize here. From a technological point of view, at the start of this period, engineering design aids consisted of slide rules, T-squares and hand-drawn blueprints, logarithmic and design tables and manual typewriters. By the turn of the century, tools such as supercomputers, desktop and handheld digital electronic devices, instantaneous communications, as well as advanced reproduction technologies, enabled engineers to improve by orders of magnitude all of the functional capabilities required for design and practice in their discipline.

The reader will discover that this narrative describes an extraordinary tale of academic endeavours that have led to world-class scholarship from members of faculty, staff and students. However it is also peppered with descriptions of some of the more spectacular student pranks carried out during this period. This is a part of the history and is not intended to condone or further encourage these activities. For example, hazing rituals that were common at the start of this period, are no longer acceptable. With pranks, there is a very fine line between what may be considered as clever and humorous and one that is unnecessarily disruptive and/or hazardous. The student reader should be forewarned that the culture has shifted significantly within the last five years and many of the escapades that are described here would today be subject to disciplinary and academic sanctions under the Code of Student Conduct. The challenge for student pranksters in the new millennium is to only engage in pranks that are creative, safe and reversible.

I have been privileged to be part of the faculty for 57 of the 60 years of its existence. First, as an undergraduate student (1957-61), graduate student (1966-69), faculty member (1968-2004) and emeritus and adjunct research professor (2004- present). As a result, I have known personally, and consider as friends, most of the people referred to in this history. Also, I have first (or in some cases second-hand) knowledge of many of the instances discussed in this book.

However, I realize there are many significant past events and accomplishments within the faculty that are not included here as there are limits to the detail space allows. I am sorry for any major oversights. Also, it is difficult to properly acknowledge the individuals – faculty, staff and students – I have met over the years, and I apologize in advance and take full responsibility for any errors or omissions.

G.S. Peter Castle, London, Ontario, May 2014

Chapter 1
The Background – Pre-1954
President G. Edward Hall

For the first six decades of the 20th century Ontario was served by only two accredited engineering degree programs, the Faculty of Applied Science and Engineering at the University of Toronto and the Faculty of Engineering and Applied Science at Queen's University in Kingston. It is interesting to note that both of the terms Engineering and Applied Science appeared in the names of these two faculties albeit in juxtaposition. In addition a few other institutions offered two-year pre-engineering programs, notably the University of Guelph, which specialized in agricultural engineering and the Royal Military College in Kingston. However in all cases, students from these institutions had to complete their requirements at either Toronto or Queen's in a traditional engineering discipline before becoming qualified to practice engineering in Ontario.

Following the end of World War II, both Toronto and Queen's were inundated with a demand for spaces driven by the influx of returning veterans. In fact, for a number of years they were forced to offer two complete programs in each academic year in order to meet this demand.

The University of Western Ontario, commonly referred to as Western even in those days, was founded in 1878. As such, it is one of the oldest in the province. In the early 1950's it was of modest size - approximately 3,000 students - and known primarily for its programs in Arts and Science, as well as Medicine and Business. The campus was in a semi-rural setting located north of the London city limits on Richmond Street at Huron Street; bound by the Thames River and the fairways and golf greens of the London Hunt and Country Club. It consisted of eight buildings: University College; Natural Sciences; the Lawson Memorial Library; Thames Hall; the McIntosh Gallery; the Collip Medical Research Laboratory; the Hume Cronyn Memorial Observatory; and the power and heating house. All of the main buildings were faced with sandstone blocks trimmed with limestone around the doors and windows in the characteristic style of modified collegiate gothic. In addition, the JW Little Memorial Stadium served as the home field for the Western Mustangs football team and doubled as the site for spring convocation ceremonies (weather permitting).

Aerial view of The University of Western Ontario, 1951. Notice the golf green of the London Hunt Club located at 9 o'clock in the picture and JW Little Memorial Stadium at 10 o'clock (Photo courtesy of Ron Nelson Photography Ltd./File photo, Faculty of Engineering Science).

Western's president, Dr. G. Edward Hall, felt expansion of the program offerings was merited, but there should be a limit of 4,000 students to maintain a quality learning environment. In 1952, he realized southwestern Ontario (the main catchment area for Western students) was under-served by professional program offerings, specifically Engineering and Law. At the same time, a small but influential group of local engineers of national stature lobbied strongly for Western to establish an Engineering program. Among them, E.V. Buchanan, retired General Manager of the London Public Utilities Commission and James A. Vance past President of the Engineering Institute of Canada (1950), who along with a number of other distinguished engineers – such as Richard L. Hearn and Kenneth F. Tupper – went on to serve as an Engineering Advisory Board to the University.

E.V. Buchanan, First Chair of the Advisory Committee for establishing Engineering at Western (London Free Press Collection of Negatives/Western Archives, Western University)

James A. Vance, President E.I.C., 1950 (Photo courtesy of Keith Stevens)

President Hall was very receptive to their views and made the far-reaching decision to initiate discussions on the feasibility of introducing a program in Engineering. With the support of Professor F. Stiling, Principal of University College, he asked Professor R.L. Allen from the Department of Physics to Chair the Faculty Committee on Junior College Engineering. Their work began early in 1953.

They soon came to the realization that in the post war years there was unprecedented expansion occurring in Canada and this resulted in a "sharply accelerated increase in employment opportunities for engineers of almost all branches of the profession".[1] In addition, it was recognized that Canada was experiencing a significant increase in university age students as a result of the post war "baby boom". In discussion with deans of Engineering from other universities (in particular, the University of Toronto and McGill University) it was learned there was a relatively high failure rate in the early years of their engineering programs.

---

1   Department of Labour, Canada, *Employment Outlook for University Graduates*, 1952.

Although they could accommodate more students in their upper years, overall capacity was limited by the large first- and second-year class sizes. Therefore, they were very supportive of the proposal by Western to introduce a 'junior' or 'pre-engineering' program encompassing the first two years, with the idea that students would complete the remaining two years at another Canadian university, such as Toronto, Queen's or McGill.

In late 1953, the decision was made to establish a two-year program administered as a department within the Faculty of Arts and Science and that "immediate steps be taken to appoint a professor of Engineering to draw up the curriculum, submit it to University Senate through the Faculty of University College, organize a teaching staff adequate to carry on the program successfully and to be responsible for the general supervision of the Engineering program". All this in addition to making sure the curriculum was acceptable to the major Canadian universities for admission into the third year (e.g. Toronto and Queen's) or fourth year (e.g. McGill) of their engineering programs.[2]

In the light of current procedures required for the introduction of new programs in universities, it is quite remarkable to realize that in a matter of months the idea put forth by President Hall was investigated, acted upon and received final approval by the Senate and the Board of Governors.

Professor L. Stuart Lauchland, then Associate Professor in the Department of Electrical Engineering, University of Toronto was a highly respected and experienced electrical power engineer. He was appointed as Professor and Head of the new Department and assumed his position in July 1954 with the hope and expectation that the first students would be admitted in September 1954.

---

2   Final Report from the Sub-Committee on Junior College Engineering to the UWO Senate Committee on Educational Policy, Professor A.H. Johnson Chairman, Fall 1953.

Chapter 2

The Beginnings – Department of Engineering Science, 1954-1960

Head, Professor L. Stuart Lauchland

When Professor L. Stuart Lauchland was appointed as the head of the Department of Engineering Science, things moved very quickly. The first major decision was the name of the department. The choice, Engineering Science, was a deliberate attempt to emphasize the practice of engineering was an amalgamation of both the art and science of the discipline. Similarly, at Toronto and Queen's University, this was accomplished by including both of the separate terms Engineering and Applied Science in the faculties' names.

However unlike the other universities where the classical engineering department structure existed, at Western, it was decided to make the two pre- engineering years completely interdisciplinary so students could defer the decision on the area of concentration until third year. This was seen as an advantage over the other programs in allowing students to make a more enlightened choice of area of specialization, following two years of experience in the fundamentals. It also had the practical advantage of allowing the curriculum to be constructed with a predominate use of existing courses in mathematics, physics, chemistry, social sciences and humanities already in place at the University. This meant the program could be offered with minimal additional staff. In fact, other than Professor Lauchland, only one other initial appointment was made. Mel P. Poucher, a young civil engineering graduate from Imperial College in London, England, was hired as lecturer to assist with the curriculum development and to teach the first-year course in Engineering Statics.

L. Stuart Lauchland, first Head department of Engineering Science
(Photo courtesy of Beta Photos).

The department was initially supplied with office space alongside Geology in the Natural Sciences Building and temporary laboratory facilities were soon established to house basic equipment, such as a small wind tunnel and materials testing equipment. The first class was enrolled in September 1954 and consisted of twenty students (sixteen of whom proceeded to second year). The tuition fee for this class was $350, the same as for students in Arts and Science. The first-year curriculum consisted of six full year courses in English, Mathematics, Physics, Chemistry and two new courses, Engineering Mechanics and a Graphics course. Lectures were given in various locations on campus as part of the regular course offerings and the two new courses were given in a lecture room in Thames Hall assigned to the department.

Class photograph of the first class enrolled in Engineering Science, fall 1954 (File photo/Faculty of Engineering Science).

In September 1955, the second freshman class of twenty-five students was enrolled. At this point, the department had to make a decision about the first class. The members of the Advisory Board strongly pushed for the establishment of a full program. The timing for expanding the program seemed right, as other universities were also responding to the increasing demand for engineers. Carlton, Guelph, McMaster and Windsor Universities were set to establish full programs, as well as the University of Waterloo, a completely new university specializing in engineering. Rather than follow the original plan of having Western students transfer to another established university, it was decided in March 1956 to extend the program into a four- year honours degree. Thus, Western became the third university in Ontario to offer a complete engineering program. Of the thirteen students remaining from the founding class, only one opted to transfer to another university (Toronto).

Members of the first graduating class (1958) attending their 55th class reunion, Homecoming 2013. From left to right: Jack (John) Bedggood, Larry McGill, Barry Robinson, Ross Judd and Rod Durnin (Photo courtesy of Adela Talbot, Western News).

The decision to offer a full program necessitated the immediate recruitment of additional faculty members to teach, develop the new curriculum and plan for housing the expanded department. John E. K. Foreman a mechanical engineering graduate from University of Toronto and Cornell was hired in 1956, followed in 1957/58 by Allan T. Olson, a mechanical engineer from Queen's University and William H. Davis a civil engineer from the University of Toronto.

This first class lost little time in making their presence known on campus both in an academic sense and as pranksters.

Surveying classes took place on campus before the start of regular classes. Shown is student Bryan Hewat, Class of 1959 (File photo/Faculty of Engineering Science).

Drafting classes were usually held Saturday mornings. Here some members of the class of 1960 seem to be involved with "bridge" design involving cards (Photo courtesy of Don Partlo, BESc'61).

Perhaps the first high profile prank carried out by engineering students came to be known as the TB Chest X-ray prank and is best described first hand as follows by Tom Collings, BESc'58:

"In our third year (1957) we acquired a wind tunnel machine. Most of our classes and labs were in Thames Hall. Four of us in Civil Engineering (Durnin, Collings, McGill and McClarty) were doing tests with it. Chest X-rays were being held at the end of the hall (four rooms away). We all had on white lab coats and had a clipboard. Students kept coming in and asking, 'Is this where the chest X- rays are being done?' Our bright idea: we told all the good-looking girls this was the right location; asked for their names and checked off the 'list.' Then, we told the girls to stand in front of the machine, put their hands behind their backs, and take deep breaths before we turned on the wind tunnel. It almost blew them out of the room! The funny thing is one-third of the girls thought they had the X-ray! We were having a great time and after about 20-30 X-rays, Professor Foreman charged into the room and put an end to our fun. He was livid, as someone had complained. He said, "Collings, if you get 49% on my course and need 50% to graduate I will fail you!" A couple of months later we had final exams. He taught Engineering 304, Heat and Thermodynamics. It was total Greek to me. I went over to write the exam at 5:00 p.m. and the room was in total darkness. The exam was held at 8:00 a.m.! I was in a total panic and went to see Professor Lauchland. I said that I had not seen the exam and asked if could I write it. He said, "No," and told me he would get back to me after he talked to Professor Foreman. They finally decided to let me write another exam after all the other exams were over. I got a copy of the original exam from my classmates and they had only changed the numbers. To make a long story short, I aced it and got an A! The only 'A' I received in my four years of university. I always tell everyone I stood fourth in my class (although there were only four in civil engineering)."

In parallel with these faculty appointments and in anticipation of the impending graduation of the first class of engineers, in 1957 E.V. Buchanan and Don Jenkins (along with five colleagues from the London area) followed the Canadian engineering tradition and established Camp 11 to administer the presentation of the Iron Ring. In the spring of 1958, Buchanan presided at the first Ritual of the Calling of an Engineer in London, a task he undertook with great pride and enthusiasm for many years to come.

The convocation ceremony took place in May 1958 and thanks to the cooperation of the weather, it was held in the open air in J.W. Little Memorial Stadium. Here, the graduating class of twelve students was awarded the first Bachelor of Engineering Science degrees from The University of Western Ontario. Fittingly, at this convocation, Edward V. Buchanan was awarded an honorary doctorate in recognition of his work in establishing the engineering program at Western. This first convocation marked the start of a pattern of expansion in the total number of graduates, coupled with variations in the choice of the different disciplines driven by student preference, and in many cases, by the job market (see Appendix 1).

During this period Professor Stuart Lauchland worked tirelessly in both developing and promoting the program to high school students interested in engineering.

Professor Lauchland's pipe

I personally recall Professor Lauchland fondly as a gentleman, scholar and all round distinctive character. One vivid memory that stands out for me is the dynamics of his discourse. In keeping with the habits not uncommon in his time, he was a pipe smoker. I use that term rather loosely, however, as his pipe was mainly a prop in support of a rather dramatic performance he had perfected. I first experienced this as a young Grade 13 student applying to Western and visiting him in his office for an interview. Any nervousness I had was soon dissipated as I watched in fascination as he tamped tobacco into the pipe in his left hand, struck a wooden match with his right hand and then began to explain in great detail about the program at Western. Both hands were used to emphasize his points and they would rarely move around together. Although I heard the words, I soon became preoccupied with two questions: first, whether the pipe would ever be lit; secondly, how low could the match burn before disaster struck. Inevitably just as he got to the main point he was trying to make, as if to add emphasis, at the last possible second he would give a flick of his right hand and in one smooth motion, extinguish the match and send it flying into the ashtray on his desk to join a pre-existing pile of burnt remnants. This was then repeated throughout the rest of the interview.

G.S.P.C.

Appointments continued with the hiring of Gordon F. Chess as lecturer in electrical engineering and John L. Kearns as associate professor in chemical engineering. This small core of seven faculty members rounded out representatives of the four disciplines to be offered: chemical, civil, electrical and mechanical. What followed was a very hectic period of ongoing curriculum development, as well as rapid planning for a dedicated engineering building that had recently been approved.

The question of curriculum was a particularly challenging task for this small group of faculty since in 1956, as the program expanded to four years, goals were set to ensure the courses offered were not simply copies of those at other universities. President Hall and his advisors prescribed they should be less oriented to specialization and give more emphasis to fundamental concepts, particularly mathematics and science. In addition, the program needed to include 20 per cent liberal arts courses, defined as being those from Arts and Social Sciences. This ideal was constrained by the need to ensure the approved curriculum met the requirements for accreditation by the Association of Professional Engineers of Ontario (APEO), namely some degree of specialization in one of the established disciplines. Additional practical details emerged, such as timetabling constraints resulting from courses offered in three-hour time blocks and the fact that many engineering courses also had laboratories associated with them. The result was a very heavy six course load, with contact hours approaching thirty hours a week – by far the most demanding at the university.

After much deliberation by a curriculum committee consisting of representatives from the university and engineering, what emerged was a distinctive curriculum that came to characterize Engineering Science at Western. The first two years were common to all students. In third year, most courses remained common, but some choice was allowed depending upon interest in one of the four options. This was followed by a fourth year, which allowed even greater specialization. The most significant characteristic, however, was the strong presence of the humanities and social science courses. Although falling somewhat short of the 20 per cent goal, the original curriculum had one full course in English, History and Philosophy in the each of first two years, followed by an additional two follow-up courses in years three and four. The program relied heavily on established, and some specially modified courses, in the basic sciences, such as mathematics, physics and chemistry. The engineering science courses included common subjects, such as statics and dynamics; graphics; strength of materials; fluid mechanics; thermodynamics; and electric circuits, etc.

In parallel with the curriculum development, work proceeded rapidly to provide the department with a new building, as the faculty offices and machine shop were temporarily housed on the ground floor of Thames Hall. To make way for the construction, the Hunt Club relocated holes 11 and 12 of its golf course. As can be seen in the photograph, this involved having more than balls getting stuck in the sand trap.

Bulldozer stuck in a sand trap on the fairway of the 11th hole of the Hunt Club Golf course, clearing the earth on the site of the current A.C. Spencer Engineering Building (Photo courtesy of London Free Press Collection of Negatives/Western Archives, Western University).

The ceremonial sod turning took place in early 1958 and, remarkably for such a major project, the building was ready for occupancy in April 1959. The cost of construction was $1.75 million and Major General A. C. Spencer of London, Ontario, gifted a total of $500,000 of this. The official opening of the building took place on Oct 30, 1959, presided by James A. Vance of Woodstock, former president of the Engineering Institute of Canada, a founding member of the department Advisory Committee, and a great friend of Engineering Science at Western. In recognition of Major General Spencer's generosity, Western's Board of Governors agreed the building should carry his name.

The Alexander Charles Spencer Faculty of Engineering Building, 1959
(Ron Nelson Photography Ltd./File photo, Faculty of Engineering Science).

For a program intent on emphasizing the science component of engineering, it is ironic this was not mirrored in the building name. The Major General insisted the word "science" not appear on the brass plaque. (This was a result of his traditionalist view of the engineering profession, but was prescient as it preceded by almost 50 years the subsequent move to change the name from Engineering

Science to simply 'Engineering' in 2001). Somewhat surprisingly, the new building was located on the opposite side of campus to the other Science departments, such as Physics and Chemistry. For a new program that was emphasizing the importance of the science component in engineering, was in fact a sister department within the Faculty of Arts and Science, and in these early years, was highly dependent upon teaching help from these other departments, this may seem unusual. There is nothing clear in the records about why this was done, but indirect evidence suggests it was a deliberate attempt to ensure the new program would develop its own character and not be unduly influenced by the other well-established programs.

Initially the building was much larger than required to house the existing complement of faculty, staff and students. A substantial portion of the upper floor was occupied by the newly established Faculty of Law and its new library acquisitions, while it awaited completion of its own building under construction across the street from the Spencer Building.

The presence of Engineering Science on campus was marked at the convocation ceremonies of 1959 by awarding of eight BESc degrees to the second graduating class, and honorary doctorate degrees to four distinguished members of the engineering profession in Ontario. These individuals - James A. Vance, Richard L. Hearn, Henri Goudefroy and Kenneth F. Tupper – were among the prominent engineers who advised the university during its deliberations on the Engineering Science program at Western. (As previously noted, E.V. Buchanan was similarly honoured at convocation the previous year.)

The year 1959 also saw the further expansion of the department's teaching complement with the hiring of professors Walter Bulani (chemical), James W. Stewart (mechanical), and George S. Emmerson (mechanical).

Meanwhile the sudden proliferation of new engineering programs in Ontario necessitated the APEO to further formalize the curriculum accreditation process though the formation of an accreditation sub-committee. In December 1959, Western's Engineering Science curriculum became the first in the province to undergo review by this committee. At this early stage the laboratories were not yet fully equipped. In addition, rather than attempt to duplicate the large-scale machinery found at traditional engineering schools, a deliberate decision was made to equip the laboratories with smaller-sized equipment that demonstrated the principles. This had the added practical advantage of saving considerable money in capital cost and maintenance. The accreditation committee raised questions about the equipment acquired for the hydraulics and heat engine laboratories. As an outcome of this visit, professors Mel Poucher, John Foreman and Allan Olson visited a number of universities in the United States to see what approaches were taken elsewhere. They confirmed the type of equipment adopted at Western was becoming the accepted approach to the university engineering laboratory experience.

In spite of those initial reservations of the visitors, the program was granted full accreditation by APEO. This meant graduates of the program were eligible to become fully licensed as a professional engineer following a minimum two years of practical and approved work experience in engineering.

Remembering the early days of the Department of Engineering Science

President George Edward Hall envisioned The University of Western Ontario to become the "Oxbridge" University of Canada, limited to 4,000 students. As a consequence, Engineering Science was established as a department headed by Professor L.S. Lauchland with a target of 400 students maximum. To his regret, President Hall was forced to yield to the public pressure of the demands for increased enrolment of students in all departments and the establishment of the Faculty of Engineering Science with Richard M. Dillon as dean. His belief that 'small is beautiful' limited the investment in the total faculty budget.

Long before Google became a verb, Bill-it or Davis-it were the two character "twitters" in the Department/Faculty of Engineering Science when any members sought academic information on students. Bill Davis, an early member in the Civil Group, had a hard-drive memory to one hundreds of a decimal point of the marks of every student he recorded in his role as Secretary of Academic Records. His talents and influence in making students and professors sharpen their memory skills deserve great respect as the faculty's own form of Google.

Walter Bulani, member of faculty, chemical, 1959-86

Paint, a gorilla mask and a missing cornerstone

Being part of the class of 1960 and also 1961, I was able to experience student life and classes in Thames Hall and later in the new Engineering Science Building. There are many incidents that happened over my time at Western University (in order to protect the innocent I will not put names to any of them):

1. Stealing the cornerstone to the new Law School the day before it was supposed to be laid in place.
2. Painting ENGINEER'S PUB OPENING SOON on the roof of the new residence building, visible to all of London.
3. We cannot overlook the Dead Horse in the Homecoming parade ending up on the Dean's lawn.
4. Walt T wearing a gorilla mask into Professor Poucher's class, which the professor ignored much to his dismay. I was riding home with Walt and it got a lot of second looks by the London public.
5. As a freshman, I played a role in the so-called X-ray machine prank.

In August of 1961 I was pleased to receive notice that I had been awarded the prize, given by the Research and Education Committee of the Canadian Construction Association for the best thesis on a construction subject. I did not know that Professor Hugh Peacock had submitted my thesis, but I was pleased to receive the prize money and an engineering handbook, which I still have after 52 years.

Don Partlo, BESc'61

Leaving their mark

Engineering '59, the second group of engineering students at Western, was small in number. Of the ten who graduated, four were in civil, four in mechanical, and two in electrical. In first year, there were only two engineering professors – Professor Stu Lauchland and Professor Mel Poucher. Lauchland who was head of engineering would often smoke his pipe while lecturing; something that was totally acceptable at the time, but would be taboo in today's classroom (not to mention illegal). Poucher was especially well liked and was noted for his extremely well organized course presentation.

While engineering students in various years of graduation delighted in a variety of pranks, the one uniquely associated with Engineering '59 was the painting of "ENGINEERING '59" in huge letters on the girders of Somerville House while it was under construction. Of course the prank was harmless since the girders would be covered when the building was finished. Unfortunately, students in some other programs followed up with their own painting elsewhere on campus in places that would not be covered up, and Engineering '59 was accused of instigating campus-wide vandalism. This unfair accusation was quickly and quietly dropped.

Jim Pleva, BESc'59

Memories drift back

I recall that we had Saturday morning graphics labs and it was informal to say the least. On one occasion, I was still in formal dress from the night before and recall falling asleep on the drafting board.

I had dinner with Tom Collings (BESc'58) recently and recalled Lady Godiva where he was the lady and I led the horse. This was followed by a discussion of the float at homecoming about the last of the dead horses (real stuffed horse in dead horse position). The dead horse then turned up on various lawns in the following weeks.

John Shortreed, BESc'60

Signs of mischief

The period of the late '50's and early '60's was marked by a notable expansion in building facilities at Western. This gave rise to some notable pranks as well. When Medway Hall was built in the late 50's, the plank roof was topped with tarpaper. Just before the final roofing was to be installed, there appeared in large white letters visible to much of London: "Opening Soon: Engineers Pub". How did the artists get up there? Legend has it a few enterprising chaps tricked an unsuspecting site guard into showing them some construction features of the new building. During the departure, key doors were tampered with so as to leave them available for entry later.

Medway Hall under construction, 1959 (Photo courtesy of London Free Press Collection of Negatives/Western Archives, Western University).

When the Law School was built, on the morning of the cornerstone laying, the cornerstone disappeared. A note arrived at the dean's office indicating the stone was being held for ransom, payable to the Red Feather Drive. The day was saved when a sharp-eyed maintenance man noticed deep tire tracks across the practice football field leading to the riverbank. The cornerstone was near the edge in the trees. The following Friday, the Western Gazette cartoon depicted a group of fellows wearing masks and Engineering jackets carrying something very heavy. In fact, the perpetrators had 'borrowed' a construction dolly for the job.

Michael McKim, BESc'61

Chapter 3

The Expansion Years – Faculty of Engineering Science, 1960-1971

Dean Richard M. Dillon

By the end of 1959 it was apparent to President G. Edward Hall that Engineering Science at Western was proving to be very successful, but also the rapid progress exceeded his expectations. Within a period of five years, a new and unique engineering program had been established and was running effectively; a highly motivated and dedicated teaching staff was engaged; and a new building was occupied. In keeping with the decision-making process of the time - no doubt in full consultation with the Advisory Committee - he decided it was time to convert the department into a faculty. Furthermore, it was believed the first dean should first and foremost be experienced in professional practice and have good administrative experience; prior academic experience could be advantageous, but not essential.

As a result, to his great surprise and understandable disappointment, in early July 1960 Principal Frank Stiling, informed Professor Stuart Lauchland on behalf of the president, that Richard M. Dillon was being appointed the first Dean of Engineering Science, effective immediately. The rest of the faculty learned of the news through a newspaper article in the London Free Press the next day. It is unknown whether this was an unintended and accidental oversight, but nonetheless it created considerable angst amongst the faculty. It was later reported the appointment and these circumstances caused more than a few eyebrows to be raised elsewhere, particularly at the University of Waterloo and McMaster University, which were developing their own new engineering programs and were

Richard M. Dillon (Photo courtesy of Beta Photos)

certainly considered major competitors for potential students. What apparently followed was a somewhat difficult transition period. As the new dean, not only did Dillon have to contend with feelings of loyalty to Professor Lauchland by the existing faculty, but also these members were very aware of the fact that he had no direct academic administrative experience.

Dillon was in fact quite a distinguished scholar, having graduated from Western in 1948 with a Gold Medal in Math and Physics. He subsequently obtained a master's degree in Civil Engineering from MIT and then qualified for and obtained his PEng in Ontario. In addition, he was a partner in the local consulting engineering firm M. M. Dillon & Co. and through this connection was also a member of the Advisory Committee to the President. In his role as a structural engineer he served for several years as a part-time lecturer in civil engineering. He knew the program well and was an enthusiastic supporter of the educational goals embodied in the Engineering Science program.

Nonetheless the circumstances of the appointment made for a rather awkward beginning both for the new dean and for the faculty. Many in the department did not previously know Dillon, even though he had taught a civil engineering course. Also, he had to quickly adapt from the familiarity of the industrial world to that of academia as it was in the 1960's. The faculty felt somewhat dismayed, as the general feeling was Lauchland was the logical person for the job and deserved it as a result of all the success he had in setting up the program over the previous six years.

It is not documented what the main expectations were for Dillon's appointment, but it appears that there were at least three: 1.) To further extend and develop the unique features of the undergraduate program in Engineering Science at Western. This offered clear alternatives to the programs rapidly developing elsewhere in the province (in addition to Waterloo and McMaster mentioned above, Carleton and Windsor universities had recently started engineering programs); 2.) Expand the program into graduate studies in selected areas of research; and 3.) Hire appropriate personnel to carry out these goals.

Dillon came into a system based upon "top down" leadership and he had full control over appointments, salaries and promotions. He recognized the existing personnel were working well together and formalized the rather loose option structure that had evolved by appointing professors Mel Poucher, John Foreman and John Kearns as "Group Heads" of the Civil, Mechanical and Chemical options, respectively, while Lauchland maintained his status as Head of the Electrical option. The faculty had a dedicated machine shop, staffed by Bill Ramakers as chief technician and Hubert Edney. There were two typists: one of whom, Edith Hall, also served as the dean's secretary.

All faculty members at this stage were fully occupied with undergraduate teaching responsibilities and the development of further courses and laboratories. As stated earlier the intent of the curriculum was to offer a unified common core followed by a modest degree of specialization sufficient to satisfy accreditation requirements and to establish a reputation for a good, student-oriented undergraduate teaching environment. As a result, all of the staff had been hired primarily because of their interest in undergraduate education, and other than Kearns, none had doctorate degrees. This was very much different than, for example, at Waterloo and McMaster where the programs were being developed in a much more traditional manner with the undergraduate and graduate programs coming on stream in parallel. In these universities it was becoming obvious that more members of faculty were being hired because of their potential in research and a PhD was more or less a job requirement. The expectation at Western was once the number of graduates increased and likewise the interest in graduate degrees, then postgraduate degrees would evolve naturally through faculty interests and the fact they would no longer be so fully occupied with curriculum development. However, Dillon recognized that it was time to be more proactive. As new hiring opportunities arose, it became possible to engage promising young engineers with a primary interest in unique areas of research, but also with an interest in the core undergraduate curriculum.

About this time Dillon learned in very dramatic terms that academia governance offered a number of additional challenges from the business world. Just as he was settling into his job and the initial awkwardness of the circumstances around his appointment was subsiding, he was suddenly put in a very embarrassing predicament by the some members of the student body. As mentioned earlier, engineering students from every university have always been known to take great pride in their tradition of carrying out campus pranks. Students at Western had embraced this with enthusiasm as witnessed by the several successful ones that had been carried out in the previous years. In this regard, Lauchland took quite a

Laying of Law School Cornerstone, from L to R, The stone being retrieved, President Hall guiding the stone in place, President Hall, Josephine Spencer Niblett and Major-General A.C. Spencer (Photo courtesy of London Free Press Collection of Negatives/Western Archives, Western University).

benign view and always expressed the belief (to paraphrase); "a good prank should be 1) funny; 2) do no harm; and 3) the perpetrators should not be found out". In the fall of 1960, a very important day for Western took place: laying the corner stone of the Josephine Spencer Niblett Faculty of Law Building (the donor was the sister of Major-General Spencer and as the building located across the street, it could literally be considered the sister building of the Engineering building). As the day of the ceremony dawned, great consternation occurred in the administration as it became apparent the corner stone had disappeared. Engineers were immediately suspect and as new dean, Dillon was put under great pressure by the president to get to the bottom of it and locate the stone in time for the ceremony. Much to his embarrassment and annoyance, other than to report receipt of a ransom demand of $50 (to be donated to a local charity), he was unable to find out anything more about it. The administration refused to consider a ransom and in desperation ordered a papier mâché substitute.[3] be made so as to not embarrass the university on this important occasion. However, about this time a sharp eyed staff member from Buildings and Grounds spotted tracks in the grass across the field behind the Law building which were made from transporting the 100lb corner stone in a

---

3   R.B. Willis, Western 1939-1970, Odds and Ends, Graphic Services, University of Western Ontario, 1980, p30.

wheel barrow and dumping it down the side of a gully at the north end of campus. Fortunately it was unharmed and retrieved in time for the formalities. This prank stretched the limits of the Lauchland's first two criteria, but the latter held and fortunately for the perpetrators, they were not found out and spared Dillon's wrath. In the heat of the moment he threatened severe reprimands, including expulsion. No doubt discovery of their identities could have had an adverse effect on a number of very successful engineering careers.

Following this diversion, Dillon began work in earnest on two fronts: the undergraduate program and graduate research.

Undergraduate Program

Dillon was a great proponent of the generalist approach to engineering education. This is perhaps not surprising for although he was a structural engineer, his own background was in mathematics and his primary interest was in management. He, along with several members of the Advisory Committee, felt the curriculum was drifting away from the concept of a "unified" curriculum.

The key to establishing Western as offering a major alternative in engineering education was to further emphasize general, rather than specialized programs. There was certainly some merit to this view as this approach had been recently adopted at UCLA in the United States and was also a characteristic of the very successful engineering program at Cambridge in England. However, the faculty was reluctant to further embrace this as result of several practical issues. One was the fact the curriculum was overly demanding, as demonstrated by the very high failure rates (not just in first year, but even extending into third year). For example, during the previous few years, first-year failure rates exceeded 40 per cent in spite of the fact that a large proportion of the incoming class had achieved over 70% on the Grade 13 Departmental Examinations. The second factor was the question of balance needed by accreditation requirements, where the professional and industrial needs demanded some degree of specialization. The existing members of faculty were adamantly opposed to any further extension into a more generalist program.

After several years of discussions no consensus was reached and the dean took another tack, suggesting an additional option that would be an "Engineering

Science" option and would be characterized as a science-mathematics-humanities stream. To this end, Sir John Baker, (later Lord Baker), professor of Mechanical Engineering and Head of Department of Engineering at Cambridge was commissioned to visit the university study the curriculum and recommend a course of action for both the undergraduate and graduate programs. This resulted in the Baker Report submitted in May 1963.

In summary, he recognized Canadian engineering education needed to be somewhat different than in the UK because generally British students entered university better prepared than their Canadian counterparts in mathematics and sciences. Also, British industry was more attuned to enabling engineering graduates to obtain practical experience on the job. As a result, he reaffirmed the approach taken at Western was perhaps the best compromise between the generalist and specialist, given the reality of the Canadian scene. Dillon accepted his hopes for a generalist option were not to be. However, it is worth recognizing that his aspiration was ahead of its time, as much of this philosophy later became part of the "Integrated Engineering" program developed in 1998 and was a first in Canada.

In late 1963, Dillon and his executive (consisting of the other Group Chairmen) decided it was an opportune time to further define the engineering program at Western. They decided to introduce an additional group - Materials Science - effective fall of 1964. G. Alwyn Geach was hired to develop the curriculum and recommend additional personnel to teach it. At the same time the faculty complement continued to expand at a rapid pace with five additional appointments in 1964, including Murray Moo Young and Kenneth A. Shelstad (Chemical), Ion I. Inculet (Electrical), N. John Gardner (Civil) and Robert K. Swartman (Mechanical). By this stage of the faculty development it was clear new faculty members were expected to contribute both to the undergraduate teaching program and graduate education and research.

Development of the Research and Graduate Programs

In parallel with his preoccupation in fine tuning the undergraduate program, Dillon worked aggressively in dealing with the second part of his mandate: developing a graduate program and hiring appropriate personnel. In hindsight, it is extraordinary to see the long-term success and significance this hiring program had for the faculty. Although not himself a researcher, he demonstrated an uncanny ability to recognize unique talent and identify research areas worth promoting. His first two new appointments in 1961- Alan G. Davenport and Larry Soderman - are perhaps the best demonstration. Both were civil engineers, but in very different areas with different backgrounds. Each worked in fields unique in engineering education in Ontario.

Alan Davenport was born in India, raised in South Africa and first recognized in the mid-1950s by Stuart Lauchland as an up and coming researcher. He was educated at the University of Cambridge and University of Toronto, and briefly worked with the Building Research facility of the National Research Council of Canada (NRC). In 1961 he was completing his PhD at University of Bristol in the emerging field of wind loading on structures when Dillon approached him about a faculty position. This inspired appointment secured Western an early, pre-eminent position as a center for what came to be known internationally as Wind Engineering. Very soon after his appointment, Davenport was successful in obtaining the first of his many research grants from the NRC (later the Natural Sciences and Engineering Research Council of Canada or NSERC) to study the effects of wind gusts on towers. This led him to establish a testing site in the field behind Spencer Hall.

Within two years of his appointment he distinguished himself (and Western) when he published "Some Aspects of Wind Loading", Proc. E.I.C. 1963. This paper was awarded the American Engineering Societies' Alfred Nobel Prize and the Gzowski Medal in Canada. There is no question that the research activities in Engineering Science were given a "jump" start through the brilliant efforts of Alan Davenport.

Larry Soderman obtained his education at the University of Toronto and Imperial College in the field of soil mechanics. He was an experienced practitioner in this field and also co-founder of Golder and Associates. In spite of encouragement from Dillon, he declined to bring his consulting practice into association with the university. Rather, he accepted a position as a part-time professor. In spite of his premature death in 1969, he pioneered the initial stages for the establishment of another area of unique strength at Western – the field of Geotechnical Engineering.

Professor Alan G. Davenport shown adjusting instrumentation on his first field experiment on the Spencer Hall property, 1961 (Photo courtesy of London Free Press Collection of Negatives/Western Archives, Western University).

The Soil Mechanics research team, 1967, Back row left to right, Professor W.H. Peacock, D. Schebesch MESc student, P.E. Bedell MESc student, Professor L.G. Soderman, R.C. Butler MESc student, R.G. Horvath MESc student. Front row left to right, S.A.Ola MESc student, Y.D. Kim PhD student, Professor R.M. Quigley, J.G. Lusk technician (Photo courtesy of J.G. Lusk).

Dillon also tried to further encourage research efforts by using some internal funds to support initial research efforts by professors Walter Bulani, George Emmerson, John Foreman, John Kearns and Stuart Lauchland.

In 1962, three more appointments were made, including Hugh W. Peacock from Toronto and Keith Upton from England who supplemented the teaching efforts in Civil Engineering, and Edwin S. Nowak from McGill University and also Purdue in Mechanical Engineering. Upton subsequently returned to England after two years and shortly thereafter Peacock was granted leave to further his education through a doctoral program in Soil Mechanics at UCLA. Nowak undertook the first major research activity in the Mechanical Group when he obtained funding to investigate the thermo-physical properties of heavy water. This was a subject of great interest in Ontario as it coincided with the development of the CANDU system for power generation, which utilized heavy water as both the moderator and coolant.

An indication of the overall research activity in 1962 is illustrated by a total research funding of $24,063, of which $13,533 was obtained through the competitive process of NRC. Two significant undertakings would have important future implications for the faculty: Davenport began the design process for the first generation Boundary Layer Wind Tunnel and Kearns submitted a proposal to the Ontario Department of Health to undertake research in the emerging field of environmental engineering. He wanted to investigate the technology of controlling emissions from coal-fired power plants using electrostatic precipitation.

Although a number of graduates from the very early years did go on to graduate studies (for example Ross Judd, BESc'58, Jim Pleva, BESc'59, Ted Aziz, BESc'60, Bob Grace, BESc'60, John Shortreed, BESc'60, among others), they all did this at other universities in Canada, Britain and the U.S. In order to meet the increasing demand for advanced study, approval for the first graduate degree in Engineering Science at Western - the MESc degree -was obtained in 1962 and immediately attracted four registrants (three of whom were Western graduates). By 1964 enrollment climbed to thirteen and the first three master's degrees were awarded to George Raithby and John Cargo, who each studied aspects of the thermophysical properties of Heavy Water, and George Steels in the field of structures. Following this successful launch of the master's program, approvals for doctoral level studies followed in 1965. The regulations for the degree were submitted to Senate and approved in 1965 and the first candidates were immediately enrolled.

The undergraduate program at Western was characterized by being one of the most demanding on campus, certainly in terms of contact hours. However students still managed to find some time on their hands as witnessed by an ongoing series of pranks. Perhaps emboldened by the publicity resulting from the cornerstone coverage, they continued to raise the ante. The most spectacular of this era was the great toilet seat caper. In the fall of 1962 a small number of engineering students spent one week surreptitiously loosening the bolts holding over 100 toilet seats in washrooms all over campus. Then in a coordinated operation over a 10-minute period they removed every one and spirited them off to a "hideaway". A subsequent ransom requested a date for an engineering student with the frosh queen. One day later all 104 seats were successfully reinstalled none the worse for wear. Dean Dillon by this time had become much more accepting of student foibles and although outwardly needing to present a stern demeanor it was reported that he too got a chuckle out of this prank that seemingly harmed no one but may have inconvenienced more than a few.

One hundred and four toilet seats and three engineering students, 1962 (Photo courtesy of London Free Press Collection of Negatives/Western Archives, Western University).

The expected increases in undergraduate enrolments in the early 1960's were not realized, mainly on account of competition from the new engineering faculties simultaneously growing elsewhere in the province. However predictions based on the growing high school population were encouraging and indicated the peak had yet to come. This is confirmed by the enrolment growth figures as shown in Appendix 2. The professorial staff steadily increased with four or five appointments each year to a total of nineteen by 1963, at which time the total undergraduate enrolment had reached 237. The Machine Shop increased its resources to meet the demand; Bill Ramakers was sent to Europe to recruit the necessary skilled staff. The Boundary Layer Wind Tunnel (BLWT1) was constructed in 1965 with the help of a grant from NRC and housed in a prefabricated metal structure provided by the university, adjacent to the Engineering Building behind the Observatory.

A sense the dynamism of this period can be sensed in this following reminiscence of Peter Teunissen, technical staff member, 1966-97:

> "It was in April, 1966 when I met a representative from Western Engineering Science in my home country of Holland. He said they had just built a Boundary Layer Wind Tunnel and needed someone who could design and build instrumentation for that tunnel. He had heard about me, he said, and then asked if I could make a traversing gear. I said, 'yes,' time and money makes everything. Well, he replied, 'I have talked to about 20 people and you are the first one that said 'YES' in a second. YOU ARE HIRED, here are two tickets and come right away.' Of course it took a little longer, but my wife and I made it to Western. My first step into the shop was quite a shock but we had to do with what was available, so, I started working. It took about a year to design and build that traversing gear but when installed with the first push of the button it went OK. The next project was the turntable. This was not an instrument, but a clunker in comparison and this worked out fine, too. We started with a whole series of model buildings, towers, two sensitive balances, bridges and finally oilrigs. The CN tower was a super structure and the highlight was the Hong Kong bank

building. During my career in the mechanical shop, I also had the privilege to work on instrumentation and equipment for many other fields of research including electrostatics, heavy water, electron microscopy, medicine and kinesiology. Over the years my work has been shown in pictures, video, film, magazines, newspaper and TV, so I feel that I have had my recognition. I am most grateful for this unique opportunity and very thankful to all my wonderful work colleagues, staff and faculty members who entrusted me to make so many of the projects that put the Boundary Layer Wind Tunnel Laboratory on the world map. I am very proud of this."

The university administration was very cognizant of the appearance of the campus and it was understood the BLWT1 facility was temporary. It was expected the whole laboratory would be moved to the new or extended Engineering Building, which was beginning to seem requisite. But very soon additions were made to the "temporary" building to accommodate the environmental engineering program, biochemical laboratories and also research activities in fluidization. The buildings ended up remaining in this spot for over 35 years.

K.F. Tupper, vice-president (Scientific) NRC, officially opened the wind tunnel on November 26, 1965, in an appropriate ceremony. It was a tool, like all special tools of this kind, which generated as much research as it could satisfy. A major part of its use, however, was to be in design consulting for which a permanent staff member was required. Nick Isyumov, a graduate of the faculty in 1960, was appointed research engineer. This was the first consulting organization to operate under the umbrella of the Faculty of Engineering Science. An important event was the Symposium on Wind Effects held on February 21, 1966 to mark the inauguration of the new facility. Forty representatives of various universities and interested researchers in the U.S. and Canada attended the event. Dillon entertained the group with dinner at the London Club. It was an exciting occasion for the faculty. The dean decided to grant Davenport the designation, director of the Wind Tunnel, the first employment of the title 'director' in the faculty. Davenport promptly received research contracts in excess of $140,000 for several projects including the dynamic behaviour of a 55-storey building for Seattle First National Bank, a 75-storey building for the United States Steel Corp. in Pittsburgh, Pennsylvania, and the wind loading of space vehicles designed by NASA. Research was also conducted on the dynamic wind loading of hyperbolic cooling towers, with the help of two graduate students.

David Surry (faculty member, 1971-2004) and Jean Surry (adjunct faculty member, 1980-2004) attended this inaugural symposium and relate this following tale that describes some of the social mores of the time that resulted in them being "bounced" from the dinner at the London Club:

"The Surry's introduction to Western happened when Dave was invited to talk about his doctoral work at the inaugural Wind Tunnel Conference in 1966. Since Jean was also a graduate student in low speed aerodynamics, she came along out of professional interest. We both duly registered and signed up for the dinner after the one-day event. When a group of us arrived at the London Club for the conference dinner, we had only just crossed the threshold when an almighty fuss broke out and we were quickly ushered into an anteroom by the manager. At that time, unknown to us, women were not allowed in the London Club and no exceptions could be made. Professor Davenport was summoned along with Dean Dillon, who were both very embarrassed. No one had connected Jean's registration with the London Club's policy. At that time, there were only about 100 women professional engineers in the country. The dean magnanimously offered to send the two of us out to dinner at one of London's finest, hosted by a surprised graduate student, Peter Rosati, who was given the keys to the dean's car and his credit card. Our destination turned out to be the old Latin Quarter, which not only provided us with a fine evening, but also set us on the road to a lifelong friendship with the Rosati family. The London Club remained a male-only bastion for some time. Its defences started to break down a decade later, when London had a female Mayor, Jane Bigelow, but initially she was only given entrance as an honorary male. It's all a little hard to believe now."

Another important development around this time was the start of the "environmental" thrust of the faculty, which evolved from the Ministry of Health's support of Kearn's proposal in 1963 to study the elimination of pollutants from flue gas emissions of steam power plants. Existing devices in use at this time for removing particulate matter employed electrostatic phenomena and eliminating noxious gases, catalytic phenomena. Kearns soon interested Inculet in this project, who had joined the Electrical Group from the electrical power industry in 1964. Kearns and Inculet broadened their interests to embrace the application of electrostatic phenomena to fluidized beds, in which work NRC supported them. Shelstad extended his catalytic process studies to include air pollution control and abatement. However, in July 1965, Kearns left the faculty for another appointment and Inculet inherited the research grant and Bulani was appointed head of the Chemical Group.

On another front, Dillon had been persuaded of the importance of the emerging field of biochemical engineering and as early as 1963 had struck a Bioengineering Committee, which included members from the Faculty of Medicine. As a result, he decided to develop research strength in biochemical process studies and lay the foundations for what became the first biochemical engineering program in Canada. At the same time, the Chemical Engineering option had uncomfortably small enrolment. It was attractive, therefore, to consider as a means of ameliorating this, a group of courses in biochemical engineering to interest engineers or chemists in the food industry, and entice employers to release suitable employees for periods of study. A specific program of courses was required and an appropriate degree would be awarded for its successful completion. The idea of a "course work" master's degree (one with negligible or no research component) had already been proposed by Soderman and the Civil Group to accommodate a similar program of courses in soil mechanics. However, the university's Faculty of Graduate Studies rejected this, largely on the grounds they did not want any of "that practical stuff," as one member expressed it, contaminating the traditional search for new knowledge at the postgraduate level. The Chemical Group, however, was not easily dissuaded and pressed for a new attempt. The Engineering Advisory Committee endorsed the scheme when it was presented to them in January 1966 and the Curriculum Committee was charged with the duty of composing a general proposal for the new degree, the MEng.

The Chemical Engineering Group planned to test the response of the food industry to their proposed MEng degree in biochemical engineering through a conference on the subject that summer. Meanwhile, professors Inculet and Shelstad pondered the possibility of a MEng program in air pollution abatement, a subject that, especially if water pollution was added, offered another attractive channel for the application of the biochemical interests of the Chemical Engineering Group. The topic of environmental pollution had recently thrust itself to the forefront of modern technological challenges. Man's abuse of his environment was forcibly brought home in many parts of the world, and not the least in the watershed of the Great Lakes. This was the era when Buckminster Fuller coined the phrase 'spaceship earth' to emphasize the finite nature of Earth's life support systems and Rachel Carson published her influential book, *The Silent Spring*. The subject became a great cause among the enlightened public and the dire warnings of concerned biologists and zoologists, which hitherto seemed to fall on deaf ears, now found a receptive audience.

As the time was propitious to mobilize science and technology for a counter-attack on pollution and to increase the awareness among engineers of the problems involved, the research work of professors Inculet and Shelstad acquired unanticipated status and the development of a whole new field of engineering study seemed expedient. In March 1966, Dillon announced the formation of an Ad Hoc Committee for Engineering Studies in Air and Water Pollution. Professor Inculet was designated chairman and along with representatives from engineering included a number of representatives of other faculties and departments - notably Physics, Botany, Bacteriology, Zoology, Geography and Law. The committee met on May 13, 1966, along with representatives of the Ontario Water Resources Commission and of the Department of Health, to discuss the type of postgraduate program best suited to the current industrial needs in the fight against pollution. The aim was to develop a structured course of study leading to a MEng degree and considerable progress was made. With one eye on this development, the Chemical Group offered an appointment to professor Jan (John) M. Beeckmans of the School of Hygiene, University of Toronto, who, on his acceptance, proceeded to conduct research into ways of improving the efficacy of air filters and recycling of incinerator ash in sewage treatment plants.

Meanwhile, the conference on biochemical engineering sponsored by the Chemical Group was held in July 1966 in the laboratories of Canada Packers, with results that were scarcely encouraging. In consequence, the group experienced no trouble in changing the emphasis of their biochemical interests from food technology to water pollution in anticipation of playing a dominant role in the creation of the proposed graduate program in Air and Water Pollution Control and Abatement, as it was now identified. Confident the proposal for a MEng degree would receive the approval of the Faculty of Graduate Studies, the pollution committee, with the energetic support of the dean, promptly submitted an application to the Department of University Affairs for a grant to help provide a 10,000 sq. ft. temporary building to house laboratories and offices for the proposed program. It was expected the program would begin in September 1967. The interdisciplinary nature of the program was emphasized - specifically the involvement of Geography, Biology, Medicine, Meteorology, Political Science and Law - which lent greater credibility to the undertaking in the eyes of the university and of the Ontario Department of Health, the most likely sponsor. The course of studies, under the title Environmental Engineering, was drawn up, quickly processed through the Curriculum Committee and formally approved by faculty council in February 1967.

Since the title Environmental Engineering was already used in an architectural connection by other institutions, some faculty members expressed preference for the retention of the title, Pollution Control. This suggestion, however, was defeated, and in this way the name Environmental Engineering was introduced to the faculty. Jim Zajic, a manager of biochemical engineering research with Messrs Kerr McGee in Oklahoma, was promptly engaged and, in April, appointed co-ordinator of the program. The MEng degree was approved by Senate in March 1967 and the MEng in Environmental Engineering was offered in the following September with an enrolment of eight students, mostly on leave from industry. The new Bioengineering building, constructed with help from the Ontario Department of Health, and located as an extension of the Wind Tunnel building was opened on December 7, 1967. This was remarkably quick work and a testimonial to the drive and conviction of the program's promoters and to the dean.

The MEng Degree

It is interesting to review the story of the introduction of the MEng degree, as the Curriculum Committee's initial proposal did not receive immediate approval when it was presented to Faculty council in September 1966. Rather to the contrary, it received heavy criticism when it was resubmitted with alterations in October. The preamble had to be rewritten and when this was completed, the revised document was accepted at the November meeting.

The main objections raised suggested the existing MESc degree would be in danger of being undermined by a competing master's degree and there was no necessity to create a rival award when there was nothing to prevent the existing degree from being offered for a purely course-work program. The persuasive counter to this was the essential requisite the MEng would be limited to the course work of one session. This made it, in effect, a one-year extension of the undergraduate curriculum. It was successfully argued industry could more easily be persuaded to free an employee for one academic year. Even more persuasive was the argument that such a program could "dilute" the content of the existing research based degree. The question of prerequisite qualifications was also contentious. Should graduates of disciplines other than engineering be accepted? It seemed inconceivable this would be relevant; a post-graduate course in engineering surely premised a first degree in the discipline (at least that is what many engineers thought), but most of the instructors were not holders of engineering degrees. In any case this was not a point, which troubled the university at large. The Faculty of Graduate Studies offered no opposition and Senate approved the MEng degree in March 1967. At this time the constituent groups of the faculty turned to considering how far the new opportunity could be exploited to the service of the community. The introduction of this degree did much to increase the total graduate enrolment in these early days and soon the number of graduates with a MEng degree was comparable to those with a MESc (see Appendix 3).

The Year 1967 and After

The year 1967 held great significance for Canada: it marked the centennial of Confederation, an event, which was celebrated in many ways, including an international exhibition in Montreal (EXPO '67). It was also the year of the new University of Western Ontario (UWO) Act and the year in which an extension to the Spencer Engineering building was planned and authorized. In retrospect it looms as a watershed in the early history of the faculty, as it does in the history of the university.

By 1966 it was clear Western's student enrolment would soon exceed the 8,000 limit accepted by President G. Edward Hall. It was clear, too, Western could not cope with this as a privately endowed university and the province was going to be more directly involved. Faculty dissatisfaction with the paternalistic mode of university government resulted in the formation of a larger and more influential Faculty Association. While this body may not have been alone in promoting the constitutional reform of the university, it was certainly its strongest proponent. The outcome of much thought and discussion was the submission of a new UWO Act to the provincial legislature in 1967. At the same time, President Hall planned to retire.

As a measure of the faculty's development and indication of modernity, in 1967 there were five typists in one central office, each appointed to work with several designated professors. Each professor, too, was provided with a telephone in that year; the group chairmen also received German-manufactured disc-type electronic Dictaphones. Most importantly, the first Xerox photocopy machine was rented and a new IBM 1130 computer was installed in its special room on the top floor. Both signified the dawn of immensely expanded possibilities. In retrospect, it is difficult to imagine how the faculty managed without them. (Prior to this the only means of document reproduction available was carbon paper typed copies, mimeograph or 3M's "Thermofax" and computers were almost unheard of for general use.)

The acquisition of the IBM 1130 was certainly a significant milestone in the evolution of the faculty. John Beeckmans was assigned the job of co-ordinating its use and hired a full time staff member to operate it, Tanya Spruyt (member of staff 1966-78, Wind Tunnel 1981-07). In her words:

> "In October 1966, Dr. J. Beeckmans took a chance on me being able to conquer this new beast called the IBM 1130. Faculty, staff and students used this computing system. Much user programming was done in Fortran. At first, second-year students keypunched their programmes on punch cards and then the punch cards were taken over to Natural Sciences Building for processing and picked up later in the day for return to the students. The disk cartridge of the IBM 1130 was the size of a large pizza box. Then Engineering added to the

system with a card reader and line printer and students could get programmes processed quickly in the Engineering Science Building. One of my main problems was trying to convince the students to take the elastic band from around their punch cards before placing them in the card reader. Once the elastic band was well twisted and stretched around a few choice parts of the reader, I would hear, 'Hey Tanya can you come and fix this.' Got to love engineers. What started out as 4K capacity went on to become an 8K capacity system. It was amazing that 8K could fill up an entire room when you think of what we have now that can fit in your pocket.

The cloakroom space on the first floor in the east wing of the building was requisitioned as a student lounge, furnished with tables, chairs and vending machines, and Room 109 at the opposite end of the corridor was converted from a storeroom to a lounge for the faculty. The faculty lounge, with its coffee-vending machine, was a great boon, providing a centre in 1967-70 for the exchange of information and opinions, which greatly facilitated co-operation, friendship, mutual erudition and greater understanding among faculty members.

Post-1967

The new UWO Act democratized the administrative structure of the university. Its provisions significantly changed the functioning of the Faculty of Engineering Science. For example, tenure rights of faculty members were legally established, and tenure and promotion committees were formed with specific terms of reference, rules and membership. A system of sabbatical leaves was inaugurated and deans and department heads (or their equivalent) were henceforth to be selected by committees of specific constitution. Their terms of office was specified as five to seven years for deans and three or five for department heads - both once renewable. Under the previous structure the dean and his executive committee comprising of group heads, which were the dean's appointees and two members-at-large elected by faculty council made major decisions. Responsibilities for recruiting and developing were largely devolved upon the group heads. Up to about

1967 faculty council meetings were relatively restrained affairs. If the group heads disputed with the dean, they invariably did so behind closed doors. In late 1966, Dillon asked for the appointment of an assistant dean and there was considerable resistance, not only on grounds of adding to the weight of administrative staff, but of further isolating him. He settled for the appointment of Professor Swartman as administrative assistant, an arrangement that lasted two years. Throughout the early life of the faculty, its effective registrar (and later secretary) was Professor Davis. His prodigious memory catalogued every student and genial presence seemed never far from the entrance hall or the adjacent faculty office. Joan Gemmill presided with what the students regarded as a reassuring maternal presence. A university committee under the chairmanship of the dean approved a system of study or sabbatical leave to begin in 1967 and of which Professor Poucher was first to take advantage.

After 1967, the exigencies of formula financing and a threatened rationalization of graduate activities in the province, as well as the requirements of the new UWO Act, called for some reorganization. This required better generation of policy and long-range planning. What followed was a period of intensified committee activity. An operations ad hoc committee was appointed in June 1968 to make the necessary administrative recommendations. This committee was comprised of the dean, and Professors Abu-Sitta, Davenport, Foreman, Swartman and Roy. Its major recommendation was the creation of a Coordination and Development (C and D) Committee, which would be responsible to faculty council for the operation and planning of all Engineering programs. This committee was formed immediately, under the chairmanship of Professor Alwyn Geach, and its recommendations on further organization were thoroughly discussed in the fall of 1968. It is interesting to note the recurring desire to establish a unique identity for the faculty was unaccompanied by any agreement as to how it was to be done. The most favoured routes were the adoption of some unique undergraduate programs and the pursuit of excellence in special research areas. Pressure was exerted towards introducing earlier specialization in several options, particularly chemical and electrical, and the introduction of undergraduate streams emphasizing management, production engineering, construction engineering and municipal engineering were under consideration.

The existing research areas in session 1967-68 were identified as:

1. Bioengineering
2. Chemical Process Development
3. Applied Thermodynamics and Heat Transfer
4. Electrical Engineering
5. Materials Science
6. Structures and Aerodynamics
7. Soil Mechanics
8. Applied Mechanics
9. Air Pollution

Notably, the word "environmental" was not used in these research areas. The feasibility of an applied research institute was also considered in the period 1968-69, but nothing came from this.

In the closing months of 1968, the reorganization of the faculty overshadowed every other consideration. The C and D Committee was renamed the Executive Committee and comprised two divisions - Undergraduate and Graduate - each with its own chairman. The chairmen were elected annually, while the group heads became chairmen of their groups for renewable terms of three years. The incumbents were re- appointed with differing periods in office so that they would not become eligible for re- election in the same year. The dean placed his tenure of office at the discretion of the faculty and a special committee recommended he begin the statutory seven-year term. He was also appointed as associate professor, since prior to this he had no academic rank. The new regime officially began with the academic year 1968-69.

On the operational side, some decisions had to be made regarding promotion and tenure criteria. A peculiar feature of the 'rank' structure at Western was the fact salary was not directly related to it. Certain salary floors were set for the enticement of new appointees, but it was not uncommon for a professor already on faculty to receive a salary below the floor advertised for his rank. As a result of intervention by the Faculty Association around 1967, this anomaly was rectified and it was agreed no professor should receive a salary lower than the declared 'floor' for his rank. There was, however, no restriction at the top, as one could receive a salary in excess of the floor of a higher rank. In the event the professor was promoted, no increase in salary was awarded. Indeed, he could be penalized by having more expected of him to warrant a given incremental increase. The earliest promotions in the faculty were justified by administrative service, but by 1967 the dean published new criteria in the Faculty Handbook for the guidance of the great influx of new members. The criteria were similar to those used in establishing salary increments with the difference that for promotion academic contributions were to carry more weight than any others. This was reiterated in 1969, while the faculty ad hoc committee on promotion and tenure made a study of the matter and the University Senate did likewise. Pending clarification, the dean took no action on promotions to full professor for two or three years, while over the same period salaries were raised by substantial amounts from a relatively depressed level.

The undergraduate curriculum, which seemed continuously under review, was subjected to intensified revision and the reputation of the faculty as one peculiarly devoted to the education and needs of the undergraduate was actively fostered. The bulk of this responsibility fell upon the chairman of the new core group, particularly in the selection of the core teaching staff and in the specification of the core curriculum. The Engineering faculty led the university in responding to student needs and in the spring 1969, quickly acted upon a Senate directive to form a Faculty-Student Task Force on Academic Programmes. This task force was chaired by George Emmerson and included both undergraduate and graduate student representatives and it produced a report submitted to faculty council in June. The proliferation of these collaborative studies became a species of overkill. Student representatives were invited to attend faculty council meetings, and then granted membership by right on the recommendation of Senate.

It is easy to appreciate governmental concern with the mushrooming costs of education resulting not only from the burgeoning student population, but also from incipient inflationary trends in the economy. The Department of University Affairs began to look askance at the duplication of special courses at the undergraduate and graduate level. To avoid direct government intervention and the proposed creation of a University of Ontario, the university presidents of Ontario agreed among themselves to attempt to make whatever rationalizations were indicated. They referred the subject of graduate studies to the Committee of Deans of Graduate Studies, which in turn, appointed committees to appraise the graduate programs of every engineering faculty in Ontario. The dean was asked by the National Committee of Deans of Engineering to report to the N.R.C. Advisory

Committee, by February 1, 1969, those "areas of research endeavour" which could be regarded as being of national significance, and to state how these particular "areas of excellence" related to priorities listed by the Science Council of Canada. The aim was to develop "aggressive programs nucleating on certain campuses across Canada". This was the first of a series of external pressures upon this relatively small engineering faculty to assert a unique niche in the mosaic of the engineering colleges of the nation and of Ontario. It was a concern, which for the next few years preoccupied the administration of the faculty. The dean reported, "the engineering research at Western is characterized by (a) the interdisciplinary nature of many research projects within the faculty and within the university and, (b) the direct relevance of their objectives to industry and society as a whole."

Of the more than fifty research projects under way at that time, 20 per cent were reported to be related to pollution control and abatement; 30 per cent to the "response of structures and environment to wind". Here was the first inclination towards what was soon to be called the "environmental thrust" at Western. No one could dispute the topicality of this subject among the concerns of the day and the feeling was perhaps the faculty's "uniqueness" could be pursued through this. The idea had much support and a director to lead the environmental program was sought and appointed in 1970. This led to the appointment of John L. Sullivan, a native of Australia, who had served in a similar capacity at Syracuse University. There was clearly momentum behind the idea of environmental engineering at Western and its devotees exerted influence to establish an undergraduate environmental option alongside the existing options.

In January 1968, the architect's plans for the extension to the Engineering Building were submitted for approval. It was a disappointment to some who had in mind some exciting new engineering college structures in England that a more imaginative break from the traditional style of the original building was not attempted. A compromise was reached which produced a comfortable if not dramatic effect. It was enough to have the additional accommodation, particularly in face of recent government pronouncements limiting new construction. The university administration made the enlargement of the Engineering building contingent upon its being shared with the Mathematics and Computer Science departments. The justification for the extension leaned heavily, of course, on the projected development plans for the faculty, which demanded much administrative effort. It was a period

47

of intense "housekeeping" activity and crystal-bowl gazing, placing considerable extra-curricular burdens on everyone. A considerable opportunity to dwell on these and to seek solutions was provided by the faculty retreats.

Extension to the Spencer Engineering Building under construction, 1970, Bioengineering building and wind tunnel shown on the right, observatory of pumpkin face painting fame shown upper right (Ron Nelson Photography Ltd./File photo, Faculty of Engineering Science).

The idea of a 'retreat' of two or three days in some sequestered spot was pioneered at Western by the Business School. Dillon was attracted to the idea and immediately saw advantages in it for his faculty in its current state with so much to talk about. The first expedition was to the Talisman Resort Hotel in June 1967 and was such a success it was repeated each year until 1970, after which time there were no funds for this sort of thing.

At this time, of the nine areas of interest mentioned earlier the major research activities of the faculty centered on the work of Professors Davenport, Soderman, Quigley, Nowak, Inculet and Zajic – Structural Aerodynamics, Soil Mechanics, Thermophysical Properties of Heavy Water, Applied Electrostatics, and Biochemical Engineering, respectively.

The first PhD was awarded in 1969. The recipient, Peter Castle, BESc'61, presented a thesis on the topic of electrostatic precipitation. He had been appointed lecturer in 1968 and following graduation was hired as assistant professor in the Electrical group. The second PhD followed soon after with Yung Duk Kim being the first doctorate to graduate from the soil mechanics group. Others were also contributing to the growing research program, but more as a secondary activity. As the faculty's emphasis towards environmental concerns became more apparent, Professor Bob Swartman developed his interest in solar energy research and Professor Foreman turned his attention to developing a program in acoustics, noise being an aspect of environmental pollution. Professor Emmerson's research interests were concentrated on Leidenfrost phenomena.

This was a period of very rapid expansion and newer members of faculty soon joined in contributing to the research efforts. Professor John D. Tarasuk was recruited in 1968 to support the heat transfer and energy conversion interests of the Mechanical group. Professor C.G.J. Baker joined the Chemical group in 1967. His special interests lay in unit processes. He soon teamed up with Professor Maurice Bergougnou (an appointee of the same period) in the development of the fluidized bed studies tentatively begun by some of their predecessors. Professor Maurice Bergougnou, educated in technical chemistry at the University of Nancy, France and the University of Minnesota, came with considerable industrial research and engineering experience obtained with the Esso Company in the U.S. Also, the Materials Science Group was quickly brought up to strength in 1966-67 with four appointments, namely Clermont Roy, who had experience in the nuclear industry; John S. Sheasby, who had interests in tribology; James (Jim) D. Brown, a physical chemist; and Ian J. Duerden, a metallurgist. They worked very hard to carve a significant niche within the faculty and the other more established groups.

Another important acquisition to the faculty in 1969 was Milos Novak, who was a visiting professor and associated with Davenport and Soderman in the field of the vibration of foundations. During his stay with the faculty, the Russians invaded his native Czechoslovakia. The Executive Committee of the faculty responded to Novak's predicament by deciding to offer him a permanent appointment, which he accepted with sadness for his forced exile, but to the honour of the faculty. Professor Barry J. Vickery, who had shown his talents within the Wind Tunnel team since 1966, returned to his native Australia in 1969 for what proved to be but a temporary absence of a few years. His return proved fortunate as it paved the way for the later arrival of two outstanding geotechnical engineers from the University of Sydney, R. Kerry Rowe in 1978 and Ian Moore in 1991.

Following the death of Professor Soderman, Robert (Bob) M. Quigley, became the research leader in the Soil Mechanics sub-group. This was the time, too, when Professors Stuart M. Dickinson (specializing in vibrations) and Terry E. Base (who had interests in fluid dynamics) were appointed to the Mechanical group. Professor Naim Kosaric was appointed to the Chemical group to supplement its strength in biochemistry.

The undergraduate teaching program was also enhanced with the appointment of Peter A. Rosati in 1967, which brought a unique flavour from Oxford and Cambridge universities, having a BA from the one and a teaching certificate from the other. He was a graduate student associated with the Boundary Layer Wind Tunnel and exhibited his exceptional teaching gifts. Professor John A. Macdonald also joined the faculty from a teaching position at the Royal Military College of Canada, and was given the special responsibility of teaching graphics and introducing a design project into the first-year course.

The statistics of this period of growth are interesting and are shown graphically in Appendix 4. About five appointments were made at assistant professor level in 1966, 12 in 1967, three in 1968, five in 1969 and three in 1970. The latter three were: Professors Kwan Y Lo, a foundation engineer from Laval University, William (Bill) Y. Svrcek a chemical engineering graduate of Alberta, whence he returned after a few years and Alan Watson, an electrical research engineer with experience in England and the U.S. who left for the University of Windsor after about seven years at Western. Each appointee had a significant place in the spectrum of talents supporting the faculty. Considerable fellowship and a strong feeling of corporate identity were enjoyed during these years and Dillon and the founding members of the faculty can be credited for this. More than one visiting professor remarked, after travels to several Ontario universities, the 'esprit de corps' and harmony of the Faculty of Engineering Science at Western was unique and well worth preserving. In retrospect, it can be seen the first phase of building the faculty was coming to an end and new circumstances were becoming apparent. See Appendix 5 for the list of full-time faculty members as of each transition of leadership.

Formula Financing

One of the major changes to the faculty was known as 'formula financing'. The formula instituted at this time for university financing accorded basic income units (BIU's) to each student depending upon the degree for which the student was registered. Then, in turn, the university apportioned each faculty its budgetary share according to its registration count.

Dean Richard Dillon and the first female student, Vicki Wheeler, 1962 (Photo courtesy of London Free Press Collection of Negatives/Western Archives, Western University).

This exerted pressure on all faculties to guard and increase their enrolments and threatened small faculties - and even small departments within faculties - with extinction should their operating cost exceed their 'income'. The Faculty of Engineering Science became very sensitive to its relatively small enrolment (about 450) compared to other Ontario engineering faculties of similar teaching strength.

Doctorate and master's students were accorded more BIU's than undergraduates, which, in turn, put a premium on graduate students. Unfortunately, few native-born Canadians had much inclination to pursue postgraduate studies. Nor did the market exhibit any particular demand for the holders of PhD's or master's degrees in engineering. A considerable influx of students from Asia, however, took up the slack. These, mainly on account of language difficulties, found job opportunities scarce and felt more comfortable in the academic research milieu. There was also a corresponding influx of undergraduates from Asia, particularly from Hong Kong, to the extent that they comprised as much as 25 per cent of freshman engineering enrolment in some universities. One interesting by-product of the BIU situation and the high- pressure competition for new students by such rivals at University of Waterloo was the faculty's bid for female students. A conscious effort to encourage women to enter engineering at Western was first made in 1967. This, of course, took advantage of the new climate of women's liberation, prevalent at the time. Some other universities did likewise, but Western was a leader in this.

The Student Revolution (1967-1970)

It is impossible to talk about this time in history without reference to the 'student revolution' occurring on campuses across North America and elsewhere.

At this time, a new social concern and awareness among the young affected all Western nations. The so-called student radicals were preoccupied with quality of life and purpose of education. They raised questions such as: was education devised only to provide human automata for the business or industrial machine; to provide expertise for the commercial manipulation of people; and to squander the limited resources of the Earth for private gain? It was perceived engineering, as an obvious instrument of technocracy, was suspect, and it was commonly believed that a high proportion of engineers and engineering students did not think about people or life as much as they thought about objects and were satisfied that technology was a great end in itself. They were certainly running against the tide, but one thing they could share with the so-called radicals was the insistence on relevance in subject matter. Few engineering students, however, saw relevance in the humanities or social sciences and, worse still, affected to despise them.

While engineering students tended to be more conservative, they nevertheless increasingly conformed to the new permissiveness in dress and conduct. It soon became very difficult for an instructor to identify with certainty at a glance the males and females among even engineering students. There was no distinguishing hairstyle and both often wore jeans. The number of girls entering engineering gradually increased and it should be noted after 1962 there was rarely a graduation class in engineering at Western, which did not include at least one woman.

The change between 1960 and 1967 was dramatic. In 1960 few students read the university student newspaper, The Gazette; by 1967 every edition was snapped up as quickly as it appeared. The issues discussed were vital and compelling and the new generation of students had new ideas; they were outspoken, flaunted sex and other taboo subjects, and were in great numbers. Almost overnight they visibly began to overthrow the established values of the first half of the century. It was somewhat appropriate the change at Western seemed to be marked by the Centennial of the Confederation of Canada. Beards were grown by many male professors and students in the fashions of Confederation Year 1867, hair was generally grown longer, and few returned to the clean-shaven, short haircut, suit and necktie appearance that once proclaimed respectability and status. In 1960, it would have been unthinkable for an engineering professor to face a class without collar and tie. By the end of the decade, it did not matter.

The last formal social function was the Christmas dance of 1966. The student dances at the start of the decade were those of the pre-war era - foxtrots, sambas, waltzes, tangos, rumbas - dances in which the partners embraced and touched. Saxophones, trumpets, piano, bass and percussion provided the music; the dress was formal and the steps clearly defined. By the end of the decade, electric guitars, organs and percussion, usually electronically amplified to extraordinary levels, formed the accompaniment of interminable free-style improvised dancing, completely informal in spirit, the couples expressing themselves to each other in random rhythmical movement far out of touching range.

In 1960 there were separate professorial, staff, and student washrooms. By 1967, washrooms were not reserved for professors, partly on account of the increased university population, but also on account of the destruction of the accepted stratifications of the previous era. The professors facing the eruption of this new breed of student had to be very flexible and adaptable to bridge the so-called 'generation gap'. The gap was always there, but now it was exceptionally wide. A lifetime of conditioning was challenged at every turn. The hierarchical authority of professors, deans, department heads, and even of the president, was brought into question. It is to the credit of the Engineering faculty that its members responded so well. One manifestation of this response was the formation of a Faculty-Student Liaison Committee, the first on campus. Since student morale had grown into a concern striking at the very prosperity of the faculty, in 1967 the teachers of the core courses were designated a core group and provided with a chairman whose primary function was to advise the dean on teaching assignments. The goal was to ensure the needs of the core instructional program were known and supplied from the point of view of teaching skills and facilities.

There was much pressure to re-examine the teacher-student relationship, even in Engineering. The blackboard was considered old-fashioned and the overhead projector was the latest teaching aid; however, there was a feeling television would conquer all. The president of the university during this time, D. Carlton Williams was known to be a strong proponent of embracing these new technologies. Professor Swartman was appointed, in 1969, to liaise with the university's Learning Resources unit and TV Council, and was given a budget to facilitate and encourage the use of the new instructional tools in Engineering. Larger classes certainly demanded new methods, but many new methods did not lead to reduced costs or even to better instruction in all cases. Many students can indeed instruct themselves from books and audio-visual tapes alone, but most cannot. All of this had to be discovered, including how much deans were prepared to fund to institute the new methods they vocally extolled. It was a period of ostentatious experimentation. The new attitudes and necessities certainly affected a revolution in the classroom. At the time, they seemed portents of the future, but in hindsight, they seem but transient perturbations in a process of a gradual build-up to a period of rapidly escalating change.

Porter and Lapp reports

The current challenge to long accepted social values, and the student revolution, conditioned academic society to questioning and change, and certainly the faculty subjected itself to a large share of both. The new UWO Act and its provision for the participation of students in the government of the university seemed appropriate to the times. So also seemed the Senate's appointment, shortly after, of what is called an academic commissioner, with a roving commission to study, consult and observe and then to report and make recommendations for changes in the way things were being done. Almost simultaneously came the announcement from the Committee of Presidents of the Ontario Universities (CPOU or COU) that they had commissioned a study of the facilities and resources for engineering education in the province with a view to recommending a role for each university college of engineering. What followed was an intensive period of introspection for the faculty as the role of Engineering Science at Western was studied from the point of view both within the University and within the system of engineering education in Ontario.

Arthur Porter, professor of Electrical Engineering at the University of Toronto and an established authority on computers and cybernetics, was appointed Academic Commissioner and began his year of residence at Western on July 1, 1969. He met formally with all faculties and bodies of the university and talked informally with everyone he could throughout his yearlong residency.

Of greater concern to the Engineering faculty, however, was the COU study. The central concept of this was to establish an integrated system of engineering education, in which each school would play a distinctive role to provide the province a variety of programs and approaches. This was entrusted to the Committee of Ontario Deans of Engineering (CODE), which appointed a task force comprising Philip A. Lapp, a consulting electrical engineer (chairman), John W. Hodgins, a chemical engineer and founding dean of engineering at McMaster University, and Colin B. Mackay, a lawyer and former president of the University of New Brunswick. The preparation of a brief for this task force was a major preoccupation of the faculty in the early months of 1970. It demanded the painstaking compilation of a multitude of statistics, details of curriculum, faculty organization, personnel, academic and professional activities, facilities and so on. The faculty devoted a whole day (April 4, 1970) to the discussion of proposed answers to the task force's questionnaire. The task force itself was present to ask and answer questions, and met with faculty in open session, as well as with the dean and some others in private. The dean and Professor Forman, the chairman of the Long Range Planning Committee, substantially compiled and edited the faculty's brief and completed the task force's formal questionnaire. The aims of the faculty expressed in these, as well as the private discussions, were of great influence on the ultimate recommendations of the task force.

After this, Dillon decided it was time to move on to new challenges as Ontario Deputy Minister of Energy. By relinquishing his office, he left the door open for a new dean to lead the faculty through whatever lay ahead. He gave notice of his intention and in the fall of 1970 machinery was set in motion for the selection of a new dean. Action, however, was delayed, pending the report of the COU Task Force, by then commonly referred to as the Lapp Report.

The final report was then distributed and its recommendation for Western was the Faculty of Engineering Science "concentrate its graduate and faculty research in the field of environmental engineering and a new common-core undergraduate program be introduced in this field in place of the existing options."[4] It also recommended graduate enrolments at the master's level should not exceed 90 students by 1973-74 and no further students be admitted to existing doctoral programs. Windsor, Carleton, Ottawa and Guelph universities were assigned similarly specialized undergraduate roles and the remaining colleges were recommended to continue offering a "full spectrum of engineering programs".

The faculty as a whole was taken aback, and did not agree with the Lapp recommendations, nor were they of mind to implement them. They had no objection to an "environmental thrust," but most saw many practical objections to the creation of a faculty of environmental engineering. Lapp too was somewhat taken aback at the vehemence of the reaction, as he felt his recommendation coincided with the aspirations earlier expressed by the faculty.

After looking over the records, it can only be concluded many members of faculty had not read the 'Statement of Goals" in the introduction of the brief

---

4   The Ring of Iron, Final report of Council of Ontario Universities Task Force on Engineering Education in Ontario, 1970.

to the Task Force. If they had, the faculty would realize they had been given precisely what they had asked for. From the brief it can be concluded the faculty was primarily interested in the development of interdisciplinary resources "for the solution of industrial problems, whether they be social, humanistic or technical".[5] For example, the faculty played a leading part in promoting a Centre for Air Pollution Studies and it was stated that "because of the fundamental relationship of biology to our physical environment, we seek to establish biology as one of the sciences underlying our study of engineering."

If a special raison d'etre had to be found for the Faculty of Engineering Science at Western, then, clearly this was it – environmental engineering. The faculty was ready to explore the idea of an undergraduate environmental stream, which had already been embarked upon; but they considered the wholesale abandonment of the existing specialties to the production of environmental engineers, unrealistic and impracticable in Canada. Even more unacceptable was the recommendation that all PhD work be abandoned. Almost simultaneously came the announcement Professor Ab Johnson, Chairman of the Department of Chemical Engineering at McMaster University, had been selected to replace Dillon and Professor Gordon Chess was appointed acting dean to administer the affairs of the faculty until the new dean could take up office later in the summer.

The first phase of constructive growth of the faculty had come to an end. It was a period marked by great expansion both in personnel and range of offerings. To put this in perspective, when Dillon took office in 1960, there were 11 faculty members and 180 undergraduate students. Upon his departure there were 45 faculty members and 451 undergraduate students. He oversaw the introduction of the graduate program offering three degrees, the MESc, the MEng and the PhD. Through key appointments he set the groundwork for many of the major fields of research synonymous with research excellence at Western, namely Wind Engineering, Geotechnical Engineering, Applied Electrostatics, Biochemical (Environmental) Engineering, and Fluidization, among others. His era saw the introduction of a completely new mode of governance, and of course, the student 'revolution'.

---

5   The Ring of Iron, Final report of Council of Ontario Universities Task Force on Engineering Education in Ontario, 1970.)

A new phase was to begin with a new dean, in the new extended premises and under new pressures and attitudes. A short period occurred in the summer of 1971 (prior to the arrival of Johnson) when Chess stepped in as acting dean to oversee the administrative details and ensure an orderly transition period.

Remembering the expansion years

Imaginative prank at J.W. Little Stadium

The University of Western Ontario was excited the 1962 Western Mustang Homecoming game was the first college football game to be televised. Students, faculty and staff were all notified of this inaugural television event, and campus police were put on high alert to safeguard J.W. Little Stadium. Yet when morning dawned on the day of the event, the words, 'Welcome engineering alumni' were marked in 10ft. high letters.

While engineers have long been suspected of capers on campus, no one has been able to prove their direct involvement. In fact, some suggested it was business students who had done this as revenge against oiled pigs being released into the business school allegedly by the engineers. "How could the campus police allow this to occur?" was the obvious question, and here the plot thickens. All the officers were at the Homecoming alumni variety show the previous evening, specifically to watch a group of 12 engineers, replete in makeup, bras, tutus and wigs, perform a hilarious version of the Bolshoi Ballet. That 12 normally square engineers would be willing to undertake this was so intriguing that all campus police left their post for 10 minutes to watch.

"We had a written invitation from the engineers to be their guests" one campus officer was quoted as saying. The perpetrators have not been discovered, although evidence included finding 50 empty bags of marking material and half a dozen lawn fertilizer spreaders near the stadium. And to rub salt into the wounds, in spite of the best efforts of the university staff to erase the message, it was still visible at the next televised game a few weeks later.

Ron Yamada BESc'64

Memories of campus

My attendance at Western in Engineering was an extremely valuable experience in terms of maturing and preparing me for my varied career. Both the academic studies and the social life were invaluable. The engineering stags allowed us to vent our frustrations, as did the pranks. For example painting the observatory orange for Halloween, borrowing the cornerstone to be placed for the law building, removing all of the campus toilet seats, and collecting and 'storing' the ballots for the Winter carnival Campus Queen particularly come to mind. The courses taught me to analyze problems and situations as I progressed through my career. Professors Soderman, Lauchland, Emmerson, Chess, Poucher, Castle and Davis, among others, were positive influences on my technical career. I made lifelong friends during my Western years; Bill Fellner, Mike Hurst, Bill Etherington, Ron Yamada, Carl Kohn, Glen Pearce naming only a few. Most importantly, I met my wife Lorraine there. Little did I know at the time how attending Western Engineering would have such a long lasting influence in my life.

John W. Jardine, BESc'65

Surveying frosh

I started Western in the fall of 1966, a green and naive boy from Woodstock. The first year I was in Sydenham residence. It was a learning experience. In the 60's, residences were not only unisex, but members of the opposite sex weren't even allowed in the door. All meals were provided, which meant a lot of walking from campus to the residence.

In first year, all 120 engineers had a common course. This created the idea of one class, which carried through all four years. At the beginning of second year, the 'civils' started one week early for surveying school taught by Andy MacKenzie, an engineer and surveyor. I'm not sure how much surveying we actually learned. It was frosh week and a great deal of time was spent viewing frosh through the levels.

In second, third and fourth year, I was involved with the Undergraduate Engineering Society (UES) serving as president in fourth year. Three of us ran, the class got together and decided whose marks would be affected the least. This serves as a good example of the practicality and caring of engineers.

My undergraduate time at Western, like most of my classmates, was hard work, a life-shaping experience and a lot of fun.

Keith Stevens, BESc'70, MESc'71, L.S. Lauchland Engineering Alumni Medal recipient 2012

Mature Student

Dean Richard M. Dillon's reply to my application in June 1963 for registration in Engineering Science was "Not accepted ...."

Immediately I drove from my home, which was an hour north of London and met Dean Dillon who explained that Professor Gordon R. Magee had rejected my application. I met Professor Magee, Head of Department of Mathematics and Astronomy, in his office in University College, who explained he rejected my application for his Mathematics course because I had been out of school for eleven years, married with two young children, and it would not be fair to my family or me that I be expected to keep up with a class of many of the brightest students in Canada.

Professor Magee continued our conversation by asking me about my experience living and working in Germany, France and Italy for four years with the Royal Canadian Air Force, after working with the Royal Canadian Air Force in Alberta and Ontario, and working in a mill and underground mine for lead, zinc, copper, gold and silver in Newfoundland. He then talked about his profession and explained teaching is increasingly more challenging each year, but the best students he ever taught were the veterans who returned to university.

This was my opportunity to say many of those veterans studied the same Department of Veterans Affairs correspondence courses, which I completed through Battersea Polytechnic Institute in London, England, to attain my senior matriculation in Mathematics, Physics, Chemistry, English, and French for entrance to university.

Professor Magee agreed that my grades were consistently high and he would notify Dean Dillon that he accepted my registration in his Mathematics course.

Flight Lieutenant (Ret.) M. Bruce Thorne, BESc'67, CD (Royal Canadian Air Force), SSM (NATO)

The alien invasion

As Professor Inculet's technician in the Electrostatics Research Laboratory, I soon got used to fabricating some pretty strange things. One of the strangest was to determine if electrostatics could be used to clear away fog.

We rented a pickup truck and built a cage in the box with an eight meter TV antenna mast that could be swung to a vertical position. At the top was a crossbar and hanging down at each end was a vertical grid about 1 x .75 meters consisting of grounded aluminum rods alternating with wires attached to a 30,000 volt DC generator. The crossbar would rotate back and forth through about 200 degrees. In order to see if the fog was being dissipated, two spotlights were mounted at the base of the mast pointing up at the grids. A portable gas generator to power the DC power supply and the lights completed the test apparatus. All we needed was a foggy night.

After about 2 weeks of taking this rig home every night, Professor Inculet called one night about 10:30 p.m. and said, "There's fog towards Dorchester" and along with Professor Castle, off we went. We set up in a little hollow on Hamilton Road just east of the bridge, about a half kilometer past Clarke Road.

It was an impressive sight! The gas generator chugging away, the spotlights shining twin beams into the sky, and the electrostatic grids arcing and snapping merrily away as the moisture built up on the frame.

Then the OPP drove up.

Apparently, some nearby residents saw the sparking and light beams and became concerned that an alien invasion might be underway! After explanations from the professor, we were allowed to continue, but asked to please inform them when we did any future test runs.

Ray Yaworski, technical staff member, 1965-73

Computer Glitches

After the Engineering Building addition was complete, we were able to have a corner in the basement behind the Mechanical Shop to install our 750,000-volt generator. And, of course, once everything was assembled, we started to do some experimenting with high voltage coronas, which would arc over at about 600,000 volts producing about a one-meter 'lightning bolt.'

In addition to engineering, Computer Science was also located in the new addition on the second floor. At this time in computer evolution (the early 1970's) computing runs still involved massive trays of IBM punch cards that often took hours to run through.

One day in the cafeteria, I overheard a group of the Computer Science students discussing the problems they were having. It seems that every so often, every computer in the department would 'freeze' and then they would have to re-start their runs.

I suspect that our arcing over 600,000 volts to a building girder (our ground) momentarily raised the ground potential which caused the computers to 'freeze,' but I didn't volunteer this information to them.

Ray Yaworski, technical staff member, 1965-73

Reminiscing the early days in engineering

When I joined the faculty in 1964 there was still resentment among some faculty because they felt Dick Dillon had been parachuted into the dean's position. But he was very enthusiastic about engineering education and supportive of engineering research. President Ed Hall had insisted the name of the faculty should be Engineering Science because there was concern in those days that engineering was too dependent on empirical formulas and had to be more science-based. First year was science (chemistry and physics), mathematics, engineering drawing and engineering mechanics and was equivalent to first-year science. The Registrar at the time suggested the best predictor of success in engineering was Grade 13 French! Typically the failure rate for first and second-year students combined was about 50 per cent, sometimes 25 per cent in each year, but more often 35 per cent in first and 15 per cent in second year.

Second year was also a common year and specialization started in third year, in chemical, civil, electrical and mechanical engineering or materials science, in a faculty comprising Groups rather than Departments. In 1968 a Core Studies group was formed to oversee the program for the first two years. Each group had a budget, but all the money was spent through the dean. I mentioned that Dick Dillon was enthusiastic about engineering education. He supported my efforts in setting up a Learning Resources Unit in the Faculty with a small amount of funding; we introduced overhead projectors to Engineering and the Western campus in the 1960s. The LRU also encouraged participation in the American Society for Engineering Education, supporting travel to ASEE meetings and guest speakers. In my mind the undergraduate program gave the Engineering Faculty its status on the Western campus in this time period.

Dick Dillon was also supportive of engineering research. He helped Alan Davenport, Ed Nowak, Jim Zajic, Bob Quigley and Alwyn Geach establish facilities to carry forward their research. The addition to the original Engineering building, now the Spencer Building, was a major project during Dick Dillon's term as dean and when it was completed in 1971, it enhanced the faculty's capabilities in teaching and research. We had to share the space for several years with computer science and mathematics (pure and applied), but could have shared it with the Faculty of Music, which would have been my preference.

Dick Dillon stepped down as dean in 1971 to become Deputy Minister of Energy of Ontario and was replaced by Ab Johnson, a chemical engineer from McMaster. Ab was a very ambitious researcher and soon received significant funding to develop computer programs simulating chemical processes culminating in the formation of SACDA. At a faculty retreat in 1971, three engineering deans were sitting at the same table: retiring Dean Dillon, acting Dean Gordon Chess and incoming Dean Ab Johnson. There was a discussion among the faculty members on the appropriate collective noun for three deans sitting together; the winner suggested by Professor George Emmerson was "an embarrassment of deans". Ab did not complete his seven-year term; he passed away from cancer after serving six years. Gordon Chess became interim dean and then confirmed for a term, but I left in 1982 before his term was completed.

It was an interesting time to be on Western's campus, with the student unrest in the late 60s preceded by the faculty unrest culminating in a new UWO Act of the Ontario Legislature.

Bob Swartman, faculty member (Mechanical), 1968-1982

The beginnings of Biochemical Engineering

It was a personal satisfaction and privilege to join Professor Jim Zajic in 1968 at the very early developmental stage of the challenging new program biochemical engineering at Western. There was lots of work ahead, and I was enthusiastic about it. Jim and I came from different educational backgrounds, he a microbiologist and I a chemical engineer, ready to start biochemical engineering.

A multidisciplinary approach to research was just at its infancy in engineering and science at that time. My goal was to combine my chemical engineering background and industrial experience with newly acquired doctoral knowledge in biochemistry – the logical outcome and new opportunity was biochemical engineering.

At that time, biochemical engineering was an entirely new addition, as no such full program existed at any university anywhere in the world. Thus, Western Engineering was at the forefront, not only in Canada, but internationally. Developing and building up this new discipline was most rewarding and challenging. New courses and curricula had to be developed on the framework of classical chemical engineering, which by itself thrived at Western. The new program was not in any competition with the basic chemical engineering curriculum, on the contrary, it added to its excellence and diversity.

A gradual introduction of this new discipline to engineering students was the strategy at that time. At the undergraduate level, students took basic chemical engineering courses, required and accredited for the chemical engineering profession. Those, who were interested in the biosciences, could choose, at the fourth-year level, to take elective courses in biochemical engineering principles. At the same time, other electives were available, such as courses in water pollution, industrial wastewater treatment, chemical and biochemical process design etc. At the graduate level, full courses were offered in biochemical engineering, food engineering, industrial wastewater treatment, biochemical process design. Special courses were developed in support of the MEng program in Environmental Engineering. Research topics in the MESc and PhD program focused on various topics in the field.

The accomplishments and results obtained within the biochemical engineering research at Western were disseminated in hundreds of scientific publications in prime scientific journals worldwide. In addition to this, many reputable scientists visited and spent extended time joining our research team. Reciprocal to this, through sabbatical leaves the Western faculty spent valuable time in leading scientific institution. In one of these sabbatical leaves at the ETH in Zurich, Switzerland, I had the privilege to join Professors Armin Fiechter, H. Ghose and E. Finn, who in 1974-75 were also having their sabbatical year at ETH. Together, we initiated the birth of the European Federation of Biotechnology, organized the first symposium in Interlaken, Switzerland and many colleagues referred to us as 'fathers of biotechnology in Europe.'

The major event, relating to biotechnology at Western occurred in 1980, when we hosted the fifth International Fermentation Symposium. The whole scientific community of about 2,500 participants spent a week at Western. Even now, whenever we meet scientists from abroad, everybody tells us that the fifth IFS was the best ever. In my opinion, biochemical engineering at Western, reached its peak that year.

There is much more to recall, during my 25 years at Western, years full of excitement, satisfaction and pride. I retired at Western 20 years ago, and have continued to be active in the field around the world always remembering the start of this pioneering program of Biochemical Engineering at Western.

Naim Kosaric, professor emeritus, member of faculty 1968-93

Professors Jim Zajic (left) and Naim Kosaric (right) looking at test sample of mushrooms growing in pulp and paper effluent, 1971 (Photo courtesy of London Free Press Collection of Negatives/Western Archives, Western University).

Chapter 4

The Introspective Years, 1971-1977

Dean Ab I. Johnson

Dean Ab Johnson was a very different person from his predecessor. He was a chemical engineer with experience in university research and teaching. A distinguished academic, he had earned degrees from the University of Toronto (BSc'46; PhD'50) and the Polytechnic Institute of Brooklyn ('48). He came to the University of Western Ontario having held academic posts at Johns Hopkins, Toronto and McMaster universities. At the latter, he served from 1962 as chairman of the Chemical Engineering department, appointed by Dean Jack Hodgins, one of the authors of the Lapp Report. It was during this latter period he turned his attention from research in the field of industrial chemical processes to the application of computers to the optimization of chemical process plant systems, a branch of what is now classified as Systems Engineering. He was in demand as a consultant with the petrochemical industries and his connections in Sarnia held promise of improving the faculty's involvement with local industry. He was both affable and friendly in manner and his reputation of having a strong work ethic and extraordinary personal energy preceded his arrival at Western. More than one member of faculty recalled being introduced to him at the faculty retreat the previous June and observing he was wearing running shoes. This was taken as a portent that everyone would have to run to keep up with him.

Johnson expected he would require administrative assistance to enable him to continue his consulting and research activities. No time was wasted in arranging for this support and two assistant deans were appointed early in 1972: Professor

Dean Ab I. Johnson (Photo courtesy of Beta Photos)

Jim Zajic of graduate affairs and Professor Peter Castle of undergraduate affairs. In addition, Doreen Dinsdale, a long-time staff member who had served in many capacities in the faculty, was appointed secretary to the dean.

The faculty not only had a new dean, but a new building. In addition, the building was shared with the departments of Pure and Applied Mathematics and Computer Science, as its new official name indicated: the Engineering and Mathematical Sciences Building. There were a number of new medium-size classrooms, as well as a lecture theatre with soft seats suitable for conferences; and large student and faculty lounges and a snack shop, as well as enlarged laboratories and office space.

Ironically, the dearth of large classrooms forced the core classes to be conducted elsewhere on the campus. Any hope of maintaining, among the students, physical identity with the Engineering building – which seemed to be important at one time – was summarily abandoned. But it was possible to assemble for special events, such as the official opening ceremony in mid-October 1971.

The principal address was given by William (Bill) M. Gauvin, Research Manager of Noranda Research Limited, supported by supplementary speeches from President D. Carlton Williams and the new dean.

Prior to his departure on leave, the former dean formed the Gzowski Society with the help of the faculty's benefactor, James A. Vance. The principal purpose of this society emerged as the promotion of an annual lecture by a distinguished engineer or scientist. Sir Bernard Lovell, the renowned English radio astronomer, gave the inaugural lecture in the spring of 1972. Lovell spoke of current developments in radio astronomy - the probing of the concept of continuous creation versus the "Big Bang Theory," and the recent discovery of black holes. On the verge of leading-edge discoveries, it was a most chastening lecture and appropriate given the circumstances.

The new dean began his term under the cloud of a sudden and unexpected drop in university enrolment, along with accompanying threats of financial cutbacks. The drop was experienced by every university in the province and was a premature manifestation of the passing of the student population bulge. This bulge had begun to congest the labour market with new university graduates, particularly those of non- professional faculties, and this turned many high school graduates away from university. The pressure on the faculty to increase government funding through the accumulation of Basic Income Units (BIUs) was suddenly in the forefront, and consideration was given to ways of enticing more students into engineering, or offering courses attracting students from other faculties. Both goals had already been explored and pursued, but with restraint. The crisis, as far as Engineering was concerned, was only temporary. The freshman enrolment soon rebounded to a record total of 223, in 1973, which continued to increase each year until in 1976 the faculty enforced a ceiling of 275. The wave of increased enrolment progressed through all years of the curriculum (see Appendix 2). This meant thought could be given to greater selectivity of students at entrance to Years One and Two, and the interest of the faculty's administrators turned from concentrating on undergraduate teaching to the promotion of graduate studies.

This period is particularly remembered as one of continuous appraisal by both internal and external bodies. There were no less than five such appraisals between 1971 and 1976. First, there was the statutory internal assessment of postgraduate studies following the appointment of the new dean; then the assessment of the undergraduate program in 1973 by the Canadian Accreditation Board which had recently re-organized and introduced new criteria to all schools across Canada. Western was the first university to experience the new revised regulations and emerged in the fall of 1973 with Full Accreditation for all undergraduate programs for the normal full five-year period. The rejection of the more extreme recommendations of the Ring of Iron, not only by the faculty but also by the Committee of Ontario Deans of Engineering, (CODE), led to a further assessment of graduate activities in the Ontario universities by CODE's Advisory Committee on Academic Planning (ACAP) in 1974-75. The upshot of this was a formal appraisal of the doctorate work of the faculty in 1976. In addition, the environmental engineering graduate program was evaluated during this period by ACAP, and internally by the university, which engaged a special consultant, professor W.W. Eckenfelder, for the task.

This resulted in approval of the faculty's work and objectives in nearly all fields, but it caused much disturbance and involved prolonged introspection to an unsettling degree. It also imposed onerous tasks upon those entrusted with assembling the data and compiling the faculty's responses, even if with all the practice it became progressively easier. Although much of the material requested had some commonality, each body seemed to require the information in slightly different detail and format. Remember, this was an era when everything was written on typewriters and electronic storage of data did not exist. In addition to these distractions, the faculty was more vocal and overtly critical of matters in council and in committee. This alone gave Johnson more difficulties than his predecessor had experienced. He was first assisted by the two assistant deans, whom the faculty authorized him to appoint, and later by an associate dean, Professor Gordon Chess. This meant the dean could attempt to continue his systems analysis activity.

With a grant from the federal government's Department of Industry, Trade and Commerce, he formed another consulting service with its own staff, but under the umbrella of the faculty and was given the acronym SACDA (Systems Analysis, Control and Design Activity). This was an obvious extension of the type of engineering innovation and entrepreneurship pioneered at Western by the Boundary Layer Wind Tunnel Laboratory. Unfortunately Johnson's activities in support of SACDA tended to place him in the posture, vis-a-vis his faculty, of a competitor for funds, space, students and research prestige, rather than of a minister to its needs. Difficulties arising from this persuaded him to resign as director of SACDA after 1975 in favour of appointing Jack Dickinson, who joined Western following a successful career with the Canadian General Electric Company in Peterborough, along with alumnus Boris Koba, who joined as a permanent staff member. About the same time, Dr. Cecil Shewchuck was enticed to join the group as a post-doctorate fellow, later to blossom as the head of the organization. This trio testified to the dean's ability to discern superior personal qualities, as well as ability. He had some success in stimulating the faculty's dialogue with its Advisory Committee, by now called the Faculty of Engineering Science Advisory Committee (FESAC), and he gave much attention to liaison with the local high schools, a duty largely devolving upon Professor Ian Duerden, who served as the faculty's high school liaison officer during these years.

Johnson also streamlined much of the administrative requirements in running what was now a much larger operation and managed to reduce the committee activity of the faculty. In addition, he pioneered in reaching out to nearby community colleges, Fanshawe College in London and Lambton College in Sarnia, in an attempt to make it easier for students who wished to transfer with some course credit into the engineering program at Western. He also attempted to increase interaction with industry, particularly in the chemical hub of Sarnia. Among other things he introduced the possibility of part-time studies by offering selected extension courses in Sarnia.

Another initiative of Johnson was that he exerted much influence to establish the 'credit' system of one-term courses. The credit system, as inaugurated in session 1974-75, was originally devised to facilitate the enrolment of part-time students and the more rapid advancement of more able students. In addition, it involved a change in the format of most lecture courses by moving away from full year courses to ones offered over the fall or winter terms, which allowed for more flexibility in the timetabling of course offerings. The introduction of these changes required considerable modifications to the regulations for progression, faculty attitudes and to the courses themselves. As associate dean, Gordon Chess ended up shepherding these changes through the various constituencies a task he managed with finesse.

The Research Environment in the 1970's

It is difficult for those now entering the research-intensive world of academia to realize engineering, well within living memory, was not a purely academic pursuit even at university. Engineering was a profession in which the practitioners united science to technology in response to the needs of society and sometimes in the creation of new needs. The engineer was essentially a designer who tried to learn from the scientific investigator the Laws of Nature as they applied to means and materials, and to develop techniques to achieve new and old practical ends with increasing ease. An engineer was not a researcher per se, although one often had to resort to research to help assess the unknown or the incalculable. No engineer was then considered worthy who had not practiced as one. Thus, the early faculties of engineering were strongly staffed by men (there were few women engineers) who had served in the design office or on the building site.

In research activity, however, the scientist (physicist and chemist) and applied mathematician have the advantage and, indeed, very often their raison d'etre. The growth of the Germanic idea of research as an essential component of education for the sciences and arts has influenced all learning activities embraced in the modern university. Until the 1950's, a PhD in engineering was a very rare qualification.

An emphasis on research was not particularly evident in the few Canadian university engineering faculties of the 1950's, but it speedily gained ground in the 1960's. At Western the examples set by Davenport with his wind tunnel and Nowak with his calorimeter were quickly followed where possible. Johnson was a strong promoter of the pursuit of contracts and research entrepreneurship supported by a staff of graduate students, postdoctoral fellows, technicians and one or two full-time research engineers. Team research activities were especially favoured - largely responding to the persuasive powers of granting agencies. Visiting professors, financed by scholarly or benevolent foundations, and part-time professors were added to the roster. The emphasis in the faculty during this period was now upon graduate studies, physical research and consulting, which was taken up with a vengeance. It may come as a surprise to many to learn the total funds from grants and contracts per engineering faculty member at Western in 1977 exceeded that of any other Ontario engineering faculty.

One by-product of the repeated appraisals was the organization of postgraduate discipline areas or 'laboratories', under three divisions, with many inter-divisional and inter-disciplinary links.

These are best described by drawing from the faculty's document prepared for ACAP in 1976.[6] Included are the names of members of faculty identified in the document as being actively involved in each area at this time:

DIVISION I:

The Boundary Layer Wind Tunnel Laboratory (Wind Engineering) - Professors Alan Davenport, Nick Isyumov, Milos Novak, Peter Rosati, Dave Surry, Barry Vickery.

The Geotechnical Engineering Laboratory - Professors Kwan Yee Lo, Bob Quigley, Kerry Rowe.

The Fluid Mechanics and Energy Utilization Laboratory - Professors Terry Base, Ed Novak, Bob Swartman, John Tarasuk

---

6   Faculty of Engineering Science submission to ACAP, June 1976.

The Boundary Layer Wind Tunnel is currently used mainly in the study of phenomena associated with wind action on structures, earthquake and other foundation forces, the dispersion of airborne particles, snow collection on roofs, and wind power generation.

Geotechnical Engineering embraces a broadly based research design and teaching program emphasizing work in (1) theoretical soil and rock mechanics, (2) soil dynamics and soil-structure interaction, and (3) mineralogical, physicochemical and geological-environmental applications. In addition to close collaboration with structural design and wind engineering, the geotechnical program is essentially interdisciplinary, interfacing especially at the research level with Materials Engineering, Geology, Geography, Biochemical Engineering and Environmental Engineering.

Energy Utilization embraces fundamental studies and practical applications of heat transfer and fluid mechanics. It is concerned with broadly based problems involving energy sources and conversion methods. Renewable energy resources such as wind and solar energy are of particular interest, as is the economical heating and cooling of living accommodation.

The Boundary Layer Wind Tunnel Laboratory and the Geotechnical Engineering Laboratory have achieved national and international stature, are well funded, and have been attractive to graduate students.

The Fluid Mechanics and Energy Utilization Laboratory has good facilities, is adequately staffed and also has attracted very good students.

DIVISION II:

Biochemical and Food Engineering Laboratory - Professors Naim Kosaric, Argyrios (Gerry) Margaritis, Ken Shelstad, V. Strizic, Jim Zajic.

Fluidization and Particulate Studies Laboratory - Professors John Beeckmans, Maurice Bergougnou.

Applied Electrostatics Laboratory - Professors Peter Castle, Ion Inculet, Nazeem Malik.

Materials Science Laboratory - Professors Jim Brown, Ian Duerden, John Sheasby, Doug Shinozaki.

This division has evolved over the period from 1966-76 as a result of interaction between some members of the four traditional Engineering disciplines (Chemical and Biochemical, Electrical, Materials Science and Mechanical). Activities of the division relate to the physical and chemical operations involved in the processing and/or separation of industrial and agricultural materials. These include mineral ores, coal, tar sands, hydrocarbons, flour, novel foods and materials of biological origin, and materials for special applications, such as heavy water. The individual members of the division have expertise in a number of domains which complement each other well as may be seen from the variety of interdisciplinary projects undertaken. Expertise has been developed particularly in the areas of fermentation, fluidization and particulate operations, particle handling by electrostatic techniques, extractive metallurgy, electron microprobe analysis, and the measurement of thermo-physical properties of heavy water. The large pilot scale fermentation reactors, fluidized beds and electrostatic processing units installed are virtually unique in a university environment.

The activities of the division have been very well supported over the years by large industrial and government grants.

The Biochemical and Food Engineering Laboratory has been the most productive of all in numbers of research students.

DIVISION III:

Environmental Assessment and Management – Professor John Sullivan.

Sound and Vibration Laboratory – Professors Terry Base, Stewart Dickinson, John Foreman.

Radio Science – Professors Zdenek Kucerovsky, John MacDougall, Alan Webster

Systems Analysis – Professors Jack Dickinson, Ab Johnson, Cecil Shewchuk.

The research areas of Systems Analysis, Radio Engineering and Environmental Studies are relatively new at Western and have as their major common element cooperation between several departments of the University.

The Systems Analysis field is based on close cooperation with Applied Mathematics and Computer Science.

The Radio Engineering Activity is carried out in close cooperation with the Centre for Radio Science, and is largely dependent on faculty in the Department of Physics.

The Environmental Assessment and Management field has operated mainly at the master's degree level, but several graduate students have undertaken research on more complex problems.

The Student Environment in the 1970s

The casual fashions and freedom from convention established by the restless and enterprising students of the late 1960s continued into the 1970s. The improved campus facilities available to the students of the 1970s were planned by their predecessors, of whom few remained on campus long enough to enjoy them. There was now the great new commodious Weldon central library; a splendid student centre, the University Community Centre, with its dining and snack areas; bookstore; offices; recreation rooms; large swimming pool; gymnasium; and beer parlour. The latter, called 'The Elbow Room' would have been unthinkable in the 1960s; Similarly, the bar in the Faculty Club, the dance and cocktail lounge in the basement of Somerville House called, 'The Spoke and Rim', and the weekly 'happy hour' of the Society of Graduate Students in the cafeteria of Middlesex College were new additions. Yet, the students of the mid-1970s were less rebellious, more concerned with job opportunities, and as a result much less exciting than their revolution-seeking predecessors.

The UWO Act of 1967 gave students the opportunity of greater participation in the academic and political government of the University. Faculty Council soon voted to invite student representatives, first to attend council meetings as observers, then to become full voting members. A system of student evaluation of professors was also formalized throughout the University. While this gave students a channel for the expression of their dislike or approval of instructors, it also gave them powers, which could be abused. Certainly this would have been regarded by professors of earlier times as intolerable, and even as a threat to professorial integrity. Prior to the formalized evaluation of instructors, many of the latter devised their own questionnaires to help improve their lectures. In 1967, the Undergraduate Engineering Society conducted teaching evaluations, but respected the professors' privacy by submitting the evaluation to the instructor and not to the administrators. The intention was to help instructors improve, and to reveal how well their colleagues scored in other courses. The new order changed this. Henceforth, student evaluations were also to be an instrument of the administration and became an important measurement tool that came to be used extensively in promotion and tenure considerations.

In the Faculty of Engineering Science, in the 1960's, much attention was given to the student, to undergraduate teaching and to the curriculum. The student liaison function of the Core Group chairman was duplicated - then superseded - through the creation of the Student-Liaison Officer in 1968 (later called Student Services Officer). This post was created to take advantage of the special qualities of Professor Hugh Peacock who was ably assisted by Jan Wolysyn in the office.

This was different than the Faculty-Student Liaison Committee, which was formed in 1966. The Liaison Committee was the first committee of its kind on campus. Other faculties followed, but the curricular and other reforms in the Engineering Faculty seem to have obviated the need for the continuation of this committee after 1970. There was also a Faculty-Student Task Force on the curriculum in 1969 and, over several years, a 'buddy' system. The latter took several forms, but essentially it was an orientation device whereby freshmen students were partnered with volunteer local professional engineers. Introductions were made during an annual dinner meeting held in the Great hall of Somerville House.

The rapid increase in enrolment in the 1970's made the idea impractical. The assurance of economic viability, which now pervaded the faculty (it no longer had an enrolment problem), had relieved it of those concerns. But, the beneficent legacy of the curricular changes made during this period is still enjoyed.

The Undergraduate Engineering Society

Around 1957, the students formed a society known as the Undergraduate Engineering Society (UES). An elected body of student volunteers has run this organization over the years.

Attempts have been made by the UES to promote a monthly newspaper, but each attempt has perished on two difficulties: the lack of sufficient writing skills, and the lack of student interest outside of their technocratic concerns and extracurricular activities. The faculty funds, which assisted the engineering students' newspaper in the past, have been withdrawn more than once on account of the paper's decline into mere obscenity.

There nevertheless have been considerable philosophical, artistic and literary talents, which have manifested among the engineering student body throughout its history, including painters, musicians, actors, singers, politicians, poets and photographers. An annual student journal was first attempted in 1967 and was repeated successfully for two years. This later evolved into an annual publication, The Onager, named presumably with great forethought, after a species of horse, known more commonly as an Asian wild ass.

A significant part of Western Engineering's history is the student pranks, several of which have already been alluded to. One classic prank was the painting of a pumpkin face on the dome of the observatory. This began in the 60's and following one misguided instance where orange and black oil based paint was used, an agreement was reached between the students and Claude Brown, the head of campus security, that if in future years water-base paint was to be used, general acceptance, albeit not tacit approval, of the prank would be tolerated.

However, there is an unfortunate tendency for pranks to go wrong. As Professor Stuart Lauchland had earlier observed, the essence of a good prank was that in addition to being harmless, the ensuing suspicion should preferably not fall on its perpetrators. Sometimes prank is not exactly the right word for describing an event.

For example, there was no doubt about the perpetrators of Superstag (as it came to be called) in 1973. It had long been the practice of the UES to conduct "stag" parties, mainly characterized by beer, cards and conversation. These were always held off-campus, the Polish Hall being a favourite venue during this era. This had the advantage of avoiding any trouble with University rules and authorities, as prior to 1967 no beer could be served on campus. In the fall of 1972, however, Dean Ab Johnson persuaded the UES representatives to plan a grand Student Conference (aka stag party) early in 1973, to which students from the neighbouring faculties of engineering - particularly of Waterloo, McMaster, Windsor and Guelph - could be invited. He thought it would be a 'coming-of-age' affair to put Western on the map. The intention was good, but the execution (as those who

A very early example of the pumpkin face on the Cronyn Observatory
dome, 1960s (Photo courtesy of London Free Press Collection
of Negatives/Western Archives, Western University).

were familiar with the students and their stags well understood) was fraught with hazards. However, everything may have passed off with but minor repercussions had it not been held in the Great Hall of the University. Some minor scrapes and spilled beer in the hall, along with painted slogans advertising Waterloo's presence and accidental (or even otherwise) displacement of the Queen's picture would not have earned the event the reputation it did, however it certainly would not have been held in the Great Hall again. Rather, the key to all the trouble arose from the presence of two young ladies who disrobed to music.

The president of the University Student Council, John Metras, Jr., unfortunately arrived at the door of the hall and was refused admission. From that point on, the event received much unwanted publicity, being duly noted in the Canadian press with many journalistic embellishments. The faculty was certainly put on the map, but not for the reasons originally intended. There was a heavy fine imposed upon the UES, ostensibly to cover the cost of damages. These damages were certainly exaggerated and the fine was largely punitive. Some credit the remarkable increase in freshmen enrolment in the next academic year to the Superstag publicity.

Superstag, 1973

Murray Black, UES president, BESc'74, recalls from first-hand experience:

> "As engineering graduates, we can remember many friends and events that we experienced during those undergraduate years. One particular memory goes back to 1973 when we had the Great Engineering Conference in the Great Hall on campus. The invited attendees were student representatives from other engineering schools in Ontario. It was the perfect academic setting, surrounded by portraits of the past university presidents, chancellors and the Queen. For this conference, the presenters we chose were not from the usual technical background, but were more gifted in the arts. To be more precise, the art of interpretive dance. Through this art form many of the delegates were truly inspired, lifting them up from the narrow outlook that was more the norm. There was such an outpouring of excitement that the

event (aka Superstag) made national news. Western Engineering was officially on the radar. Enrolment went up considerably the following year giving the faculty a significant boost. Thinking back I don't think Vice-President Adlington ever showed his appreciation. Perhaps it was an oversight on his part."

The Final Year Banquet

Throughout the years, the Final Year Banquet was something of a ritual. Two third-year students, one of whom chairs the occasion, organize it. A speaker is usually invited and the several Undergraduate Engineering Society prizes are awarded.

The first few of these occasions during the 1960's were held in the Iroquois Hotel, but it was moved to other locations in the city, such as the Holiday Inn. Once a few students, clothed and unclothed, jumped in the swimming pool and an unnamed professor successfully raced a student across the length of the pool. Along with the holiday dance, it was one of the most enjoyable student occasions on the calendar in the 1970's.

Student Technical Night

The Student Technical Night is another annual event that has grown into an institution over the years. The ES 400 final year project proved to be an educational device of considerable force. This was a full year course that challenged students to engage in a significant design project carried out under the supervision of a faculty member. The topic was very flexible and could be suggested either by the student or the supervisor. The intent was to utilize knowledge gained from the previous technical courses and to produce a significant final formal report that was presented in both written and oral form. During this period the projects could be carried out either by an individual or a team of students. An example of the latter was the successful urban car, "Urbine," and can be best described by alumnus Keith Zerebecki, BESc'72, MESc'73, the student team leader:

"The urban car, aka 'Urbine', named such due to the hum of the electric motor which gave it a unique whine, was the one of the first major competitions the engineering school entered. In all there were over 50 universities from the U.S. and Canada that spent more than a year designing and building a two passenger urban car, and brought their vehicles to the GM Proving Grounds in Detroit for inspections, analysis. The runoff competition road test took place August 6-11, 1972. Western, in partnership with Fanshawe College, scored the highest of all vehicles and was awarded the overall winner in the electric car category. The citation reads, "for overall excellent performance in all tests and for high degree of student effort in design and construction". UBC was the overall winner with a beautiful gasoline powered vehicle. (None of the electric vehicles attained the required 50-mile range, while our batteries were drained after 47 miles. (Darn. So close.) The University of Toronto was awarded the 'Most Innovative' vehicle, as they entered with an AC electric vehicle. Well Done Canada!"

Urbine was an exceptional example of a fourth-year project. There was a time when it was feared the increasing number of students and the strain upon the originality of their ideas, the ideas of the professors and the physical resources would present insuperable difficulties to mounting suitable projects, but this has not proved to be the case. On the contrary, over the years this project has become a highlight to showcase the range of student creativity and hard work. In the seventies, the three projects gaining most favour in the selection system were presented before three adjudicators invited from the engineering profession on the Technical Night. The evening also included musical entertainment, which thanks to the organizing skills of Professor Hugh Peacock made this an entertaining, as well as edifying evening.

The End of an Era

The academic year 1976-77 saw Professor Stuart Lauchland's retirement. The event was marked by a dinner organized by engineering alumni and held in the London Club, and included a gathering of members of the University and of the profession

Plague for "Urbine," overall winner in the electric category of the North American Student Urban Vehicle Design Competition 1972. Design team from Western and Fanshawe College consisted of K. Zerebecki, K. Philbrook, C. Zajc, H. Koba, P.Tam, S. Yu, A. MacDonald, B. Lloyd, and R. Shanklin (File photo/Faculty of Engineering Science).

and organizations to which he contributed. An award in Lauchland's name was announced; a medal to honour distinguished contributions to engineering by an alumnus or alumna of the faculty. It was a milestone for the faculty, as this was the first retirement and Lauchland was the first faculty member to be elected President of the Association of Professional Engineers of Ontario (APEO). Since then a number of these medals have been awarded to deserving individuals (see listing in Appendix 8).

Johnson's tenure was unfortunately marked by a loss of fellowship and corporate identity within the faculty. One would have thought the threats to viability and the increasing financial constraints would have closed the ranks within, but this was not evident. Perhaps the physical divisions of the building and the increased size of the faculty and student body, and perceived conflicts of personal interest, conspired to produce a centrifugal effect.

Some faculty members of this time suggested that Johnson's release of the machine shop from the control of the Faculty was a symptom of this. He, very understandably, found its management onerous and its budgetary demands an increasing problem. When an opportunity arose for the machine shop to become part of the University's services and be administered by the central authority, he was eager to take it. The reluctant acquiescence of the faculty was procured on the expressed understanding that if it did not work out well, the act was reversible. There were many rumblings of unhappiness at the separation of the shop, an essential component of a Faculty of Engineering Science, from the responsibility of those it served. In the spring of 1977, the new administrators of the faculty's machine shop dismissed Raja Geadah, the model-maker of twelve years service, as redundant. While the dean was parrying the protests of those most concerned, Bill Ramakers, the creator and head of the machine shop for eighteen years, was dismissed on the same grounds. These events led to heated faculty council meetings and remained a point of contention within the faculty.

Regrettably by 1976, Johnson looked anything but well. He was proud of the fact hitherto he had never had a day's illness in his life; but something was now obviously wrong. He was somewhat discomfited to receive the diagnosis of a rheumatic condition. With no relief of his symptoms, further examination revealed the devastating news that he was suffering from advanced cancer of the gastro-intestinal tract. For Johnson, aged 53, the news must have been especially catastrophic.

He valiantly conducted his affairs as usual. A pall of concern and compassion for a brave colleague in dire distress fell upon the faculty, a pall that intensified as he visibly declined but continued in the execution of his duty. No problem seemed too small for his attention. It was a sobering and affecting experience for everyone in the faculty, particularly demanding of the people closest to him.

Some members of faculty compassionately proposed the prompt institution of an entrance scholarship in the dean's name as a gesture of honour and to mark his retirement. Arrangements were speedily made, with the dean's approval, and a presentation ceremony held in the presence of a capacity audience of his colleagues, friends, relatives and students. In a uniquely solemn moment, he expressed his appreciation through a microphone discreetly held in his cupped hands, acknowledged many old friends and thanked everyone. He said he enjoyed an interesting life and his heart was full. He died a few weeks later. As a further blow in this tragic year, Jack Miller, a preceptor and administrative officer for Johnson, also died.

The faculty soberly went about its business again under its well-tried manager, Associate Dean Gordon Chess. After due process by the dean's selection committee, Chess accepted the appointment of dean, and led the faculty into the last quarter of the 20th century.

Looking back through the Johnson years

Professor J. E. K. Foreman

Several memories of John and his work come to mind. On the research side, he had a great personal interest in sound and vibration. He worked with many companies and outside Western organizations, such as the City of London. His noise surveys, analysis and report lead to the City's noise bylaw, which is still enforced today. We can all remember his big, bright yellow 'Sound and Vibration' van, ever ready to be deployed on the next mission. On the teaching side, he was our leader. He not only taught us the technical course content in a very effective and focused way, but also taught us very precise written communication skills. Every word had a purpose. Each word was carefully chosen. Several iterations and drafts were reviewed and refined until the concise message was crystal clear. As it turned out these communication skills were more valuable than the technical ones.

Keith Zerbecki, BESc'72, MESc'73

No smoking

In the 60s and 70s, smoking pipes or cigarettes were popular with academics. Students smoking anywhere in the engineering building was forbidden and certainly not allowed in the classrooms. However, a few members of faculty were known to actually smoke while lecturing (a feat in itself) and the majority smoked in their offices and in the classrooms where we met for council meetings. At these meetings the air was normally thick with foul smelling smoke. Most smokers were the senior faculty but many younger ones felt they had free license to emulate them. I would sit in the back of the room beside an open window and even still I would develop a serious migraine. I had to find a solution. Out of desperation prior to the next scheduled council meeting, I walked into the empty classroom and wrote 'NO SMOKING' across the width of the blackboard.

About thirty minutes into the meeting, the chair was asked if the 'no smoking' sign was for real. There was a long pause and finally the dean said, "I think so". No one ever smoked again during faculty council meeting and I never let on to anyone that I wrote the sign.

J.D. Tarasuk, Mechanical faculty member, 1968-2000

Building a solid foundation

It was in 1973 that I started my career as an engineering manager after graduation from The University of Western Ontario with a BESc degree. The engineering education I received from Western gave me the foundation to build a successful business career that grew beyond practicing the discipline of engineering. Like most undergraduate students, I really didn't have a clear vision on which technical discipline could be most advantageous for me. The broad based education approach at Western Engineering including the opportunity to take courses outside of the engineering discipline, such as Business 20 and Speech 101, was very beneficial in supporting my career aspirations throughout my career. As a foreigner when I arrived at Western, in many ways the four years I studied at Western meant more to me linguistically and culturally than getting an engineering education.

THE *Write up Front* ENGINEER *Write off*

OCTOBER 19, 1972   UNIVERSITY OF WESTERN ONTARIO, LONDON, CANADA   Volume 15; Number 2

evaluation - conclusion

In this age of political polarization and rapidly disintegrating channels of communications, one wonders if the old methods of initiating changes should be rejected in favour of the far more radical and disruptive methods employed by the young crusaders in the streets.

Last March, the U.E.S. council had to decide its course of action after it learned that the faculty had rejected the idea of making their course evaluations available to the Dean. Since student-faculty relations tended to be a bit shaky by the end of the school year, the council decided to let the issue cool down for the time being. During the summer though, the council distributed an evaluation questionnaire to various engineering professors in the hope of providing, for the students, an explanation of

A crowd of approximately 350 students watched the final game McLarty of the Canada-Russia Hockey Series in the student lounge. The seismic activity generated by their victory cheers is reported to have cracked plaster in the building and disturbed several computer science majors who were studying at the time. EXTRA VALUE EDITION

Excerpt from *The Engineer*, Oct. 19, 1972 (File photo/Faculty of Engineering Science).

Some say that our memory is made up of a collage of snapshots of unique events. It is certainly true in my case when I try to recall my four years at Western. I saw snow for the first time in my life while waiting to catch a bus on Richmond heading to the campus. I received my first failing mark in a second-year electronics course mid-term examination from Professor Bonnema. At graduation, I received the Julien C. Smith award. That was a pleasant surprise. I used the $400 cash award to visit my brother in Calgary, the first family member I had seen in four years in Canada.

My involvement with Western Engineering had a sequel. In late 1990s and early 2000s, I was fortunate and got involved with the Engineering Science Advisory Council for close to ten years. It was satisfying for me to have the opportunity to give back to the faculty. During my time on the Council, the faculty went through some trying times. Under the leadership of Dean Mohan Mathur, with the support of Western President Paul Davenport and many alumni and community members, the faculty started on a course of reinventing itself, refocusing and rebuilding. Today, Western Engineering is well known nationally. It has a reputation of innovativeness and graduating high quality engineers.

Henry Yip, BESc'73, L.S. Lauchland Engineering Alumni Medal recipient, 1998

Where were you in '72 when Paul Henderson scored "The Goal"?

Well about 350 students, staff and faculty were crowded around a 20" (really big in those days) TV in the cafeteria that afternoon of Sept. 28, 1972. What a roar when Henderson scored! Nearly took the roof off our new addition. Likely a few classes were were missed that afternoon. What a moment.

Keith Zerbecki, BESc'72, MESc'73

Western Engineering leaves a life-changing impression

My memory of the four years at Western Engineering is unforgettable.

Leaving home in Hong Kong at age of 18 and going directly to Western was a big change. The climate, classes, school mates, social life all needed major adjustment. Fortunately I received lots of help from professors, friends and classmates. By the second year, I felt at home learning how to live and 'work' independently, yet enjoying a good social life. Then it was summer jobs in restaurants and hotels, school in the fall and winter. I came to Canada with the plan to go back to Hong Kong to pursue business and make my fortune! Sometime in the second or third year, the Canadian lifestyle became irresistible and I decided to become a citizen and stay. With this sense of being in my new home, my best year was the fourth.

After graduating I went to the University of Toronto graduate business school, but the highlight of my university career is Western. I enjoyed it so much that I talked to my son Brian about it when he was growing up so he went to Western too, studying both Engineering and Law. I did not make a fortune, but I have really enjoyed working and living in Canada.

Tim W. Kwan, BESc'73

Women in Engineering, 1970s and 1980s

I dropped out of second-year engineering in 1972 for family reasons. By 1974, I wanted back. So, naively I just walked in the Engineering Office at Western, and asked to get back in. Joan Gemmill was there; she made it happen. I was in, including credit for all my first year courses!

In retrospect, I know that there should have been a LOT more hoops to jump through. No doubt she worked through the Dean's Office to get it sorted out. I graduated with the 1978 class. I worked at a few places, starting with a job that Professor Surry helped me find. I moved along into the aerospace sector, then into the space sector - including work on the Canadarms.

But it's only in the last few years I realized I owed Mrs. Gemmill a big 'thank you.' I liked Western, so I went back yet again. I had worked for a few years in London. I started a part-time master's degree. Then I changed jobs and moved to Toronto. Western worked out something so I could take a couple of courses through University of Toronto's Institute for Aerospace studies, to complete my course requirements.

While I was pregnant seemed a good time, to finish off my thesis Dr. Vickery was my thesis advisor – he's a nice, succinct kind of guy. I did the experimental work in the wind tunnel. After my baby was born I was operating mostly back in Toronto finishing off my thesis. The night before my defense coincided with Western's fiscal year end. As I was transmitting my final thesis and presentation copies from Toronto, the entire Western computer system went into some sort of year-end lock down. I was pretty panicked – aggravated by typical postpartum sleep deprivation. Somehow or other, the wind tunnel staff sorted through my problems, and I got the transparencies I needed for my thesis defense.

Sherry Draisey, BESc'78, MESc'87.

Working at Western Engineering

My 42 years at Western began in early 1962 with my first position being a technician in the Engineering machine shop. At that time the Soils Lab was in its early stages of development. My role in the shop was to design and build some of the first apparatus required for the lab. As the Soils Lab expanded, I began working half time in the shop and half time in the lab and ultimately became the full time Soils Lab Technician. As time went on, I managed numerous labs within the Geotechnical Department until my retirement in 2004. My time at the university gave me the opportunity to work with many members of the faculty and staff, as well as undergraduate and graduate students from all over the world. This was a very rewarding experience from which I gained many friends.

My recollection of my first experience in the field was the day my supervisor, Professor Larry Soderman, asked that I meet him at a bridge on Sunningdale Road where we were to meet a driller who would be drilling and taking soil samples. That was it – no other instructions! I decided it best to take along borehole log sheets and something to write with. After I arrived, Larry drove up in the station wagon he used to transport his little league hockey team and it was littered with everything imaginable, including candy wrappers. The drilling was underway and Larry was logging soil samples on one of those candy wrappers. He handed it to me, told me to carry on, as he had to leave. I was somewhat terrified. Guess that's what they mean by baptism under fire! As time passed, I became well aware of Larry's outstanding abilities as a Geotechnical Engineer and gained considerable respect for the man – both professionally and personally. We lost him too soon.

Professor Hugh Peacock asked me to build a bench top model quick sand tank to demonstrate the principle of quick sand. This model became a fixture in the Soils Lab where it remains and is still used today. It has always been one of the most popular demonstrations enjoyed by kids of all ages over the years. When I realized this model was such a success, I thought it would be fun to build one large enough to sink a student in. My "quick sand tank" allowed a student to stand on stable sand that supported them without a problem. Once I turned it to quick sand, it would lose its strength and would no longer support the student - they would sink to the bottom! This tank was a never-ending source of amusement for students and visitors.

During my 42 years at Western, I was privileged to work on many large Engineering projects. A few of the more memorable projects supervised by Professor K.Y. Lo are: Heart Lake Tunnel; Darlington Generating Station Intake Tunnel under Lake Ontario; Windsor-Detroit Tunnel; and Wallaceburg Silo Testing. Space does not permit describing many memorable stories from these field trips. Suffice it to say that there were some scary moments involving water and explosives!

Gary Lusk, Geotechnical Engineering staff member, 1962-2004

Students sink into the quicksand tank (Photo courtesy of Gary Lusk).

Chapter 5
The Stable Years, 1977-87
Dean Gordon F. Chess

Dean Gordon F. Chess came into his position well seasoned in the ways of the faculty and university. He was active in teaching in the undergraduate program of the electrical group since his appointment in 1958. In mid-career he developed an interest in biomedical engineering and completed his PhD through part-time studies at Worcester Polytechnic Institute in 1974. Throughout his career he showed interest and abilities in administrative duties, having contributed more than his share of efforts to committee work both within the faculty and on behalf of the faculty in Senate committees and sub-committees. As well, he served two earlier interim terms as acting dean. An associate dean during Johnson's tenure, Chess carried much of the load in administering the undergraduate program, a task that had become particularly onerous as the growing pains of the credit system were sorted out. As Johnson's illness became more debilitating, he also shouldered many of the normal decanal responsibilities.

Chess undertook his new full time deanship responsibilities very seriously and set aside any personal aspirations from his recently developed research career to devote his efforts to streamline teaching duties and help his colleagues to expand their research programs. He also had a special rapport with the undergraduate students. Although his military experience had given him a reputation of being a strict disciplinarian and a "no nonsense" type known for following rules, he was also known as a kindly gentleman who treated his students with affection and respect. In particular, and somewhat surprising to some, he had a soft spot for student

Gordon F. Chess (Photo courtesy of Beta Photos)

foibles and was known to both forgive and look the other way when circumstances merited it. Previously as Group chairman, he opened his home on many occasions to entertain student groups for evening get-togethers where "all could be revealed" but "nothing was reported". On the other hand, he was quite capable of making his concerns known when the boundaries were pushed, as was sometimes the case with certain student behaviors of this era.

Chess did a lot to further encourage female participation in the engineering program, where possible. One initiative involved inviting a local engineer, Jean Surry, to accept a non-stipendiary adjunct affiliation to help female undergraduate students adapt to engineering culture. In this activity she worked closely with Doreen Dinsdale, administrative assistant to the dean, to further promote women in engineering through a program they called "Women in Engineering, Science and Technology" (WEST). This program is still active (2014) and now is known as Women in Engineering (WiE).

If the earlier years of the faculty development were characterized by rapid expansion and innovative opportunity, Chess' tenure was a very different story. The faculty complement had grown to a size that was considerable and stable, ranging from 43 to 46 during his deanship (see Appendix 5) but was less than optimal for the number of students enrolled. In fact, the undergraduate enrolment had more than doubled in the period 1972-73 to 1978-79 (see Appendix 2), but the university resources committed to the faculty as a percentage of the university budget remained essentially unchanged.[7] As enrolments continued to increase in the early 1980's, there was absolutely no opportunity for new appointments. This resulted in increasingly unsatisfactory values for the student-to- faculty ratio, a measure widely used in universities to quantify faculty workload and quality of student instruction. Throughout the early 1980's, data shows Western had one of the highest student-to-faculty ratios of any engineering school in Canada. Certainly these years were very difficult economic times as recessionary conditions were being experienced in many countries. Canada was particularly hard hit and by 1981 the triple whammy of extraordinary high rates of inflation (12%), interest rates (21%) and unemployment (13%) put serious constraints on all levels of society and particularly university funding. These were the conditions faced by Chess,

---

7   Long Range Planning Committee report, Faculty of Engineering Science Apr, 1982.

particularly for the first four or five years of the decade. As a result, there was virtually no opportunity for change and he found himself in the role of trying to maintain morale in the face of the constrained resources.

Evolution of the Curriculum

As a result of his previous experience as acting dean, both prior to the arrival and after the death of Johnson, and also as associate dean during half of Johnson's tenure, Chess had intimate knowledge and interest in the undergraduate curriculum. The program started in the early days with a common curriculum for the first two years of all options. In the late 1960's, both the Chemical and Materials Groups successfully argued they needed one course exception to the common curriculum in the second year due to the special requirements of their disciplines. With the introduction of the credit system in 1973-74 and the division of the four-year program into eight terms, the common courses became limited to the first three terms, with two of the six courses in term four being discipline-specific for all five options.

One of the great strengths of the engineering program at Western was the strong support received from other departments throughout the university. This was not found at many engineering schools and the interdepartmental support, along with the core program, helped maintain the unique flavour of the Western program for students. However, Chess recognized that as the fields in engineering were changing even more rapidly, there was increasing pressure to introduce some change. There was real difficulty in including all the material in each discipline as desired by industry and as prescribed by the Canadian Engineering Accreditation Board (CEAB). In order to include the necessary topics and still maintain reasonable course loads (still the highest of any program in the university), by 1985-86 the program was changed and only the first two terms remained common. The full second-year program became specific to each discipline, albeit with certain common courses, such as applied mathematics, computer graphics and statistics. This adjustment did not affect a key advantage of the Western program: students did not need to choose their field of study until second year. Over the years this had proven to be very attractive to students, as many of them upon entering university had no real understanding of what was involved in each area of specialization.

The common first year not only included the important core courses, but also an orientation course to the profession of engineering that included descriptions of the five different Groups. His role as dean did not preclude Chess' involvement in teaching and he impressed both his colleagues and the student body in electrical engineering as he continued to teach a lecture course and was regularly found helping out in the associated laboratory. In this regard he was unique among his decanal colleagues in Engineering Science.

Research Activity

Notwithstanding the difficult economic times of this period, the faculty's research activity and productivity continued to thrive. In keeping with the relatively small size of the Western program, the faculty's strategy of concentrating efforts in selected and specialized research areas led to expanding recognition both nationally and internationally.

Space does not permit a full recounting of all of the innovative research activities in place during this period, but perhaps it is appropriate to present a 'snapshot' of the different areas of strength, as summarized in the dean's annual report's to Western's president from the period 1978-83:

Applied Electrostatics
Biochemical and Food
Energy and Heat Transfer
Fluidization and Particulate Studies
Geotechnical
Materials Science
Radio Engineering
Sound and Vibration

In addition to these academic research activities, which involved the efforts of an impressively high percentage of active faculty members, there were three groups involving a large component of permanent staff supported by external contracts, including the Boundary Layer Wind Tunnel Laboratory, Systems Analysis and Control Activity and the Multi-disciplinary Accident Research Team.

Boundary Layer Wind Tunnel Laboratory

Previous mention has been made of the innovative research carried out at the Boundary Layer Wind Tunnel Laboratory (BLWTL). Since the construction of BLWT1 in 1965, Prof Alan G. Davenport led a talented team of engineers and technical staff to gradually expand the scope and scale of the work carried out in the facility. The wind tunnel had a very special relationship with the Civil Engineering Group, as some of the researchers were full-time faculty members and several of the hired engineers had part- time faculty appointments. The achievements of this group were pioneering and many major tall buildings, bridges and other large construction projects from throughout the world were tested for their wind loading characteristics in this original tunnel. As a result, Western was widely recognized as being the leader in the field of wind engineering. It was apparent to Davenport that in order to maintain this leadership role, it was necessary to expand the wind tunnel facility. But the early 1980s was not a time to look for much financial help from the faculty or university. This scenario is best described by alumnus Peter King, BESc'73, MESc'78, PhD'01, who has served as director of the BLWTL since 2000:

> The 1980s were a busy time for the BLWTL. Alan Davenport, Dave Surry, Nick Isyumov, Barry Vickery, Milos Novak, Terry Base and Raouf Baddour received a large NSERC Grant in 1981, for the new 'Second Generation Boundary Layer Wind Tunnel,' which would have twice the wind speed, twice the cross-sectional area, two test legs (a high speed and a low speed test section) as well as a wind-wave tank – a truly multi-purpose facility. The grant was well short of the estimated $2.9 million required for a new building to house the new wind tunnel, office and classroom space, workshops and room for the existing 1965 wind tunnel, which had been the workhorse for the first 15 years of the BLWTL. Many projects such as the Halifax Narrows Bridge, CN Tower, Sears Building in Chicago and the Hong Kong Bank were tested in this first-of-its-kind facility.

The NSERC Grant was supplemented with funds provided by the Ontario government with a BILD grant, Western's Second Century Fund and BLWTL Reserves, bringing the total up to just over $2 million. Although already begun, the project was in danger of stalling or being cut back drastically without the addition of additional funds. With some more money from BLWTL reserves, as well as another NSERC Equipment grant to fund the wind/wave operation of the new wind tunnel, I was hired as a full-time research associate to design the turntable, roughness elements, low speed floor and wave paddle as well as to oversee the commissioning of the facility. I know that an additional equipment grant from NSERC was sought the next year and was awarded, but at a level that was less than what was required. At that time the Hong Kong Bank was finishing up the tests in the old wind tunnel facility BLWT1 in the Biology Building and the client was so impressed by the work that was being done and the savings that was realized in their new headquarters building in Hong Kong from undertaking the wind tunnel studies, that they very generously provided by a top-up of the funds needed to see the completion of the new wind tunnel – building included. The bank had requested that the amount of their donation be kept confidential, so suffice it to say that it was most generous and quite unexpected but just what was needed to get us to a point where the project was a definite "go" in its entirety. These were the days of successful NSERC Infrastructure and Operating grant applications that were needed to see the commissioning of the facility, iron out some of the bugs and to enable the facility to be a fully operational "second-generation" wind tunnel.

The grand opening was on May 14, 1984. An open house was held, with tours of the new facility provided for guests. The old wind tunnel had not been moved to the new facility as yet and many of the items mentioned above had not yet been installed, but the open house was still a significant event in the mid-80s. Some Hong Kong Alumni were here and together with the Hong Kong Students Association on campus provided a colourful 'Dragon' ceremony, in which a large dragon danced and cavorted in the 'Galleria' or central display area of the new building. A memento of the occasion remains to this day as a dragon kite with a 10 meter long tail adorns the ceiling area of the space.[8]

SACDA spinoff

After Johnson's premature death, the academic component of the systems engineering program gradually disappeared from the curriculum in the early part of the decade. On the other hand, the contract research group he started (which was subsequently expanded by Jack Dickinson and Cecil Shewchuk) became an independent company SACDA Inc. in 1986 and became such a thriving entity it moved out of Western to a new location on Dundas St. in 1993.

This was the faculty's first major commercial spin-off and still one of the most successful. The impact of this both within and outside the university cannot be underestimated. It is certainly not co-incidental President George Pedersen first raised the concept of a Research Park at a meeting of the Faculty of Engineering Science Advisory Council, (FESAC) in 1985. He received enthusiastic endorsement not only from the members of FESAC, but also the faculty and eventually other departments, particularly in the Faculties of Science and Medicine. This was to be a facility to nurture new companies with support from various departments at Western and to encourage this interaction was built on university property immediately adjacent to the campus on the northwest corner of Western Road and Windermere Road The first building, named after former Graduate Studies Dean Gordon J. Mogenson, was opened in 1989 and was soon followed by Windermere Manor, a conference centre and hotel complex in 1991.

---

8   For a complete story of the wind tunnel and the immense contributions of Alan Davenport, refer to Siobhan Roberts' book, *Wind Wizard: Alan G. Davenport and the Art of Wind Engineering*, Princeton University Press, 2013.

Multi-disciplinary Accident Research Team

This was a research initiative began in 1974 by Professor Ed Nowak, with the support of Transport Canada and involved investigating the causes and resulting injuries from car crashes occurring in the London and District area. During this period the team was particularly active and researchers worked closely with local police and medical authorities, producing annual reports aimed at identifying automobile design issues, as well as driver failures that resulted in car crashes and injuries. The researchers came from different backgrounds and were supported by contract funds.

MEng in Environmental Engineering

Engineering Science at Western pioneered the discipline of environmental engineering in Canada. One of its more visible components was the successful MEng program emphasizing air and water pollution issues. However, by the late 1970's and early 1980's many other universities followed this lead and were actively supporting and promoting similar programs. In spite of valiant efforts by director John L. Sullivan to expand the program in order to compete with other offerings, it became clear Western's enrolment was sub-critical and financial constraints caused the program to be dropped in 1983. However this did not affect the ongoing academic research activities in the faculty as projects aimed at various environmental issues existed and continued to expand in each of the active research areas listed above.

Departmentalization

Structurally the Western program was unique in Canada due to the fact there was no organization based upon departments. This had evolved from the early history of the faculty where the options were offered within a Group structure and the administrative and much academic control was centered in the Dean's Office. Over the years, on periodic occasions, discussions had taken place on the limitations of this arrangement. One of the repercussions of the adoption of the credit system was the added complexity and responsibilities for program management. Chess recognized this and, along with the Group Chairmen, engaged in much discussion about the pros and cons of changing. The traditional view presented by some was the Group structure was unique to Western and represented an important part, not only of its history, but more importantly the pedagogical philosophy that encouraged common courses and interdisciplinary collaboration. However, practical issues related to administrative workloads, efficiency and effectiveness of interactions with the undergraduate student body finally persuaded the Dean's Council to propose a departmental structure be adopted. This was agreed to by Faculty Council in 1985 and subsequently received the approval of both the Senate and University administration. As there were clearly some budgetary issues involved, it was agreed a transition year would be followed by full implementation in the academic year 1986-87. After ten years in office and several terms as acting dean, Chess announced that he planned to retire from administrative duties and return to full-time teaching, so this change was conveniently timed to coincide with the upcoming appointment of a new dean who would have the opportunity to start afresh under the new organization.

Student Pranks

A common theme occurring throughout the terms of all the deans is the student propensity for engaging in attention-getting pranks. However, Chess' tenure was a period of great activity for such shenanigans. This is not to say he actively encouraged them. Rather, it says more about the playfulness of certain members of the student body of this period, particularly those in the late 1970's and early 1980's. Each year's 'prank team' seemed driven to outdo each other in terms of originality and level of daring. It is fair to say Chess was perhaps somewhat more understanding of this aspect of student life than his predecessors. Both Deans Dillon and Johnson were barely able to disguise their displeasure and embarrassment at the more egregious of the student efforts in this regard.

It is impossible to properly document all of the various pranks which took place during this very active period, however some of the more memorable include the following as summarized by alumnus Ed Beange and enhanced with some added detail provided by some of the perpetrators:

Prose, Pranks and Fish Tanks

"I treasure my memories of the time I spent at Western Engineering during 1975-1979. I have kept many of the friends I made in Engineering, despite them being spread across the globe. I have organized every reunion since graduation and look forward to these events. Recently we attended the Celebration of Life of Greg Bryan, BESc'79, where I realized how deep these friendships are buried into my soul.

The Engineer

"I was editor of The Engineer, a so-called 'technical journal' for three years, having apprenticed under another editor in first year. Once each month we would gather in the engineering cafeteria, type up articles, paste up the pictures, drive the pages to the printer and distribute them across campus. More often than not, Mrs. Dinsdale would search me out after publication date and Dean Chess and I would have a heart to heart talk about our indiscretions and the "smut" that we were printing. I came to know the dean quite well, so well in fact that he was the first to recognize and vocalize that "I would never amount to anything in life".

"I remember fondly the many pranks and activities that I took part in or observed being planned and executed. The line between a great prank and vandalism is a fine one. Usually it was perceived as vandalism if campus security interrupted you halfway during the execution and a fine prank if you were stealth enough not to get caught.

Some 'successful' pranks:

Homecoming Brick Wall

"A group of engineers ordered a load of cement bricks and cement to be delivered to the shipping/receiving area of the engineering building. They had bricked up all of the entrances to the Law building and were on the last door (the tunnel doorway) when campus security arrived. Fortunately, the bricks were returned to the shipping area, so the creative minds went to work on this opportunity. Ours was the third or fourth float of the homecoming parade. We let off a smoke bomb at the bridge (we had previously found the formula for smoke bombs that would fill city blocks with smoke), put a steel cable across the road and built a brick wall complete with cement and left the rest of the parade sitting on Richmond Street, tying up traffic for hours.

Smoke bomb on university bridge during Homecoming Parade 1979
(Photo courtesy of Ed Beange).

"Blocking the bridge became an annual event moving from Homecoming time to the night before the Iron Ring ceremony. Various years competed to outdo the previous year in terms of speed of erection, height etc. One particularly impressive one in the early eighties as reported in the London Free Press involved "65 engineers with 150 cement blocks, eight plastic garbage pails of mortar, four trucks, four cars and a football, about 4 minutes to block the 33-foot roadway to a height of four feet and shut down the entrance for more than an hour. And finally, as a sign of the times, the engineers allowed women to take part for the first time. They played football and slung mortar with the best of them."

Bricked up entrance to campus during Homecoming, circa 1980 (Photo courtesy of Ed Beange).

Winter Week log cutting contest: Brain beats brawn

"The Western Student Council decided to hold a log-sawing contest at the student union building as part of Winter Weekend. They phoned all of the faculties pretending to be another faculty and challenged everyone to a showdown. This is one of the cleanest pranks that came off well; no vandalism, no one got hurt and we didn't insult anyone. After the go signal, we started using a hand saw like everyone else. I think it was Dino Paron who started the chain saw outside and as he brought it through the emergency stairway, it sounded like a plane taking off. We beat the other faculties, most notably the MBA's who brought in these huge guys. We got half the beer prize, and the fastest team with the more traditional manual approach won the other half.

Log cutting contest; Ed Beange is wielding the chainsaw
(Photo courtesy of The Gazette/File photo, Faculty of Engineering Science).

Big Ball on Campus

"I don't know where we got the idea or the ball, but we inflated this huge cloth ball and started rolling it around campus. It took on a life of its own as we rolled it through all the buildings, put it on the university tow truck, and played soccer and volleyball with it.

The cloth ball bounces around campus (left) and on the tow truck (right)
(Photos courtesy of Ed Beange).

Golf Tournament

"I didn't think the indoor golf tournament would amount to much, but it was inclusive with faculty getting involved as well. The course ran down hallways, stairs, through elevators, lecture halls and I think there was a hole in the Dean's Office reception area. We dressed up in silly costumes and golf clubs ranged from hockey sticks to vacuum cleaners. This started in the late 70's and became an annual event. See below for a description of the 1982 and 1983 versions.

Dean Chess' Fish Bowl

"The reception area of the Dean's Office was lined with industrial plastic, filled with water and then filled with gold fish preventing the Dean from getting into his office. I am not sure what the purpose of the escapade was, but it sure took a long time for campus security to figure how to get the water out of the bowl.

Homecoming Football Stadium

"Our plan was to put ENGINEERING '79 on the football field. We drove out to Exeter to a CO-OP store to buy lime, snuck it over the fence in the middle of the night, and then realized we had nothing to spread the lime with except our hands. We ran out of lime after ENG and by game time the grounds people had turned our artwork into large smudge.

Parked Car

"Over the years another classic prank has been to relocate cars throughout the campus by "parking" them in bizarre places that have included half way up a lamp standard or cut in half and then welded around a lamp post and other similar attention getting locales. Prank Team '80 was particularly creative when in their attempt to celebrate Western's 100th anniversary year they managed to position this vehicle between the first and second floors of the Social Sciences building.

Prank Team '80 and their memento to Western's 100th anniversary celebrations in 1978 (Photo courtesy of London Free Press Collection of Negatives/Western Archives, Western University).

"In hindsight, I think many of the pranks were done because we wanted to be recognized and validated. Regardless of our motives, the planning, the failures, the trips to the police station and campus security offices – and the occasional successes – brought us closer together."

Ed Beange, BESc'79, President, Hansen Industries Ltd.

As mentioned, the annual indoor Golf Classic became a tradition during Dean Chess' term and it became a highly anticipated event for faculty, staff and students. Each year brought new challenges to the 'course' and the level of zaniness never ceased to amuse. The following description, as provided by alumnus Bill Nickle, former UES president, BESc'84, shares highlights over several years:

G. F. Chess Golf Classic 1982-84

"The G. F. Chess Golf Classic was a welcome break each February from studies and long, cold winter days. The golf tournament took place within the walls of the Spencer Engineering building, perhaps in recognition of the building's location on the original London Hunt and Country Club's golf course. It was assumed the Engineering building was constructed on the 19th hole.

The organ grinder and monkeys are, from right to left: Sheila MacFarlane, Don Hockin, and Scott McKellar, in 1984. The last two monkeys are unidentified (Photo courtesy of Sheila Nickle).

"The nine-hole course played throughout the building, across multiple floors, requiring skillful shots down corridors, ramps, and stairways. For studying students, it was not unusual to have a golf ball bounce by as golfers "played through". Putters were recommended, to minimize damage to walls and ceiling tiles, but any form of 'club' could be found in player's bags.

"Dean Gordon Chess awarded the trophy to the lowest scoring foursome, although it was obvious that more competition went into the costumes donned by the golfers."

Bo Peep and the sheep are: Storm Purdy, Bill Nickle, John Reid and Johan Martensson in 1982 (Photo courtesy of The Onager, 1982/File photo, Faculty of Engineering Science).

The lady with the big follow-through is Nina Lowes in 1983 (Photo courtesy of The Onager, 1983/File photo, Faculty of Engineering Science).

Middlesex College Tower

Aside from the annual ritual of painting a pumpkin face on the dome of the Cronyn Observatory, the Middlesex College clock tower proved to be the most challenging site for engineering pranksters and became the subject of two of the most spectacular pranks ever mounted at Western.

The first occurred in 1977 and involved specially "rigging" the chime control of the clock to ring 1280 times consecutively. In order to do this, unnamed students had to reconnoiter the interior of the clock tower. They apparently did this ahead of time by convincing the unsuspecting janitorial staff that they were studying clock mechanisms as part of a project and wanted to see one first hand. In the course of accessing the site, they passed through several doors and were able to 'adjust' the locks to enable after hour's entry.

The following article that appeared in the student newspaper the Gazette perhaps best describes the event:

Let the bells	**The Gazette**	ring out

Volume 86, No. 11　　　THE UNIVERSITY OF WESTERN ONTARIO　　　September 16, 1977

Middlesex College gets its bell rung

by Tom Nunn
Gazette Staff

It was 1,280 o'clock according to the bell in Middlesex Tower, Wednesday.

The bell rang 1,280 times consecutively from noon until 12:50 before a timer, placed in the tower by mechanical engineers, put the clapper to rest.

"It took two hours to get through four steel doors," said one of the five engineering students who broke into Middlesex Wednesday night.

The engineers said they hooked a relay switch, battery and clock to the Middlesex tower bell so it would ring 1,280 times, for 50 minutes, every twelve hours. "We also left a sign, Mechanical Engineering '78."

"Toll them that the bell tolls for Claude Brown, Western's chief of campus security," said another of the engineers. Engineering students built a five-foot brick wall across university bridge during exams last year. Brown was quoted in the Gazette saying Security had been tipped off that a brick wall would be built and next time the prankster would be caught.

"We were not aware of this prank at Middlesex, because if we had been, we would have stopped them", said Brown. Some minor damage had been done to the doors but a full report had not been made, he said.

"From here on, the engineers and I are a little bit at odds". Brown said. "If it had been any other students, I would consider it a prank".

Brown said Security found the engineers sign but "whether or not the note is a true authentic note, we don't know". "All we have is a note inside the area saying Mechanical Engineering '78." It could be a group of

social science students, he suggested.

Bill Rowley, superintendant for buildings and grounds at physical plant, estimated the total damage at less than $75. A door was damaged but most of the cost will be labour costs to have electricians fix the tower clock mechanism.

"This is probably the least damaging prank we've had around here for a long while", said Rowley.

Rowley was not optimistic that the pranksters would be caught but Brown said security has several avenues to gain information

"Last year, I requested that the engineering society look after the cost rather than laying a charge against the man caught and they didn't even answer the letter", he said.

"I have to check on whether the man is at school and, if he is, we will take him downtown to lay charges." he said.

Brown was also optimistic that security would gain more information regarding the prank "It's surprises me how many people are on our side at times."

It is quite possible for someone to get into Middlesex College during the day or night because "most areas here are open", said Brown.

"We have some areas wired for sound but we can't afford to have all areas wired", he said.

The engineers said they had been planning the prank for six months, since final exams last year.

Associate Dean of Engineering, Dr. D.F. Chess, said "anyone with electrical knowledge could do that kind of thing". "We don't teach them anything about clock-making here."

LET THE BELLS RING - Several engineers look on as Middlesex Tower bell rings during lunch hour Wednesday. The bell rang 1,280 times after five engineers hooked a timer to the tower clock mechanism. (Nunn(

Excerpt from The Gazette, Sept. 16, 1977 (File photo/Faculty of Engineering Science).

However, there is no doubt one of the greatest pranks has to be the Mickey Mouse caper. This daring and spectacular effort required two attempts as described in the following submitted by Bill Nickle, UES president, BESc'84:

The placing of a Mickey Mouse face on the Middlesex College clock was one of the more famous pranks pulled-off by the engineers. Photos of the stately clock tower with its amusing face made it into newspapers across the country, including the front page of the Globe and Mail. The prank was really a simple statement of what the engineers thought about the "Artsy" side of the campus. But it was no simple exercise and it took several years to accomplish.

In 1979, the freshman class of '83 discovered a large plywood Mickey Mouse face in the Undergraduate Engineering Society's office. It had been constructed by a previous class with the intention of adorning the Middlesex College clock, but for reasons never revealed (common sense?) the prank was never completed. A hard-core group of Class of '83 students then made it their mission to carry out what their brothers had started.

Plans were put in place to avoid security, access the tower, and lower a man on ropes to position the clock face. Ah, the best-laid plans of [Mickey] mice and men often go astray. It was very early on a windy morning and it proved very difficult for a person dangling on a rope to control a two-meter diameter sail. Worse, the mission was planned 'on the hour' and with the minute hand pointed to 12, there was no room to maneuver Mickey under the hands and into the recessed area of the clock face. A female 'jogger' had been positioned as a sentry to alert the team if campus security should come by. Unfortunately, it did not occur to anyone that a woman out running very early in the morning might appear suspicious to security and the sentry had the unintended effect of attracting attention. The man over the wall was hastily pulled back up (which was a good thing since there was not enough rope to safely lower him to the ground) but in doing so he got snagged on a ledge at the top of the tower, causing excessive pressure on his groin and his cries pretty much guaranteed security's attention.

The pranksters all survived and lived to see another mid-term exam. Mickey, however, was arrested and put into lock-up. He was however 'sprung' from security during the ensuing year (it was an inside job) and he made his way back to the engineers.

In October of 1980, a much wiser group of mouseketeers made a second attempt. Two people went over the top this time, with longer ropes. The time was 6:30 a.m. and with both hands of the clock pointed down, Mickey slipped on the clock face easily. And there were no female joggers attracting attention. The rest is history.

Two views of Mickey mounted on the Middlesex clock face, long perspective view (left) and close-up view (right). (Photo courtesy of London Free Press Collection of Negatives/Western Archives, Western University)

Baptism of the Engineering Student: Class of 1987

"One of the great Orientation Week traditions was to have the frosh gather for a 'class photo.' The students would dutifully line up outside the Engineering building in rows, all smiles for their first group photo as engineers. Then, on a count of "1, 2, 3...smile!" garbage pails full of water would be dumped from above on the unsuspecting frosh. They were now baptized.

Class of '87 and the "water dump" soaking
(Photo courtesy of The Onager, 1984/File photo, Faculty of Engineering Science).

"Since this was an annual event, it is amazing the deception was pulled off without more suspecting students. Perhaps it was because once one had been initiated, the secret was kept in order to share in the shame of being soaked. Or perhaps some frosh knew it was coming and wanted the experience, or at least needed the shower. In hindsight, we probably should have cleaned the garbage pails first.

"The best location for the photo op was in front of the doors to the patio behind the Spencer building. The parapet directly above made a perfect place to hide a crew with pails of water. However, access to the roof happened to be through the Dean's Office. For the record, the dean never gave his permission for anyone to crawl through his windows (and I learned an important lesson about when not to seek permission), but he did seem to be conveniently away at just the right moment.

"On at least one occasion, the pranksters themselves were pranked. The second- year students behind the parapet failed to recognize there was another roof above them. As they celebrated their successful soaking of the freshmen, they received their second baptism from senior classmates. They should have known by now that water, and seniority, flows from the top down."

The second-year water dumpers are re-baptized
(Photo courtesy of The Onager 1984/File photo, Faculty of Engineering Science).

Bill Nickle, UES president, BESc'84

However not all student activities were focused on pranks and attention getting stunts. Some combined elements of the two in instructive and innovative ways. As an example, the late 1980's saw the start of a unique competition that continues to this day. The challenge to engineering student teams across the country: construct and race a toboggan made of concrete.

Western students took on this challenge with enthusiasm and the photo below shows one of the first designs to be raced. Needless to say, the designs have become more streamlined over the years.

Members of the concrete toboggan team, Feb. 1986, pushing the "brass" on a test run. In the toboggan from left to right: Professor Hugh Peacock, team advisor; Professor Mel Poucher, Chair Civil Group; and Dean Gordon Chess (Photo courtesy of Alan Noon/ Communications and Public Affairs Collection/Western Archives, Western University).

Here are some more personal reminiscences of this era:

SACDA

How many companies can you name that were university spin-offs, have thrived for over four decades, and today have nearly $100 million in annual revenue? One of the few anywhere in Canada would be Sacda Ltd., started in the early 1970s by Dean Ab Johnson in the Faculty of Engineering Science. SACDA (Systems Analysis Control and Design Activity) started out as a Centre of Advanced Technology within the faculty. Its staff primarily researched and developed simulation and optimization technology (regarded as rather esoteric at the time) for industrial applications.

A key product developed was TRAINER, an operator training simulator system used for training process operators, similar to the flight simulators used in aviation training, but for the safe and efficient running of processing plants. After Dean Johnson's death, Jack Dickinson became director and continued with the strategy of innovative technology development. The group eventually became a spin-off of Western in 1986 by Cecil Shewchuk, director at the time, and was subsequently acquired by Honeywell in 1992. Today, the company located in downtown London still employs many graduates from Western Engineering, whose first jobs after graduating were with Sacda Ltd.

Acquisition of SACDA by Honeywell Inc. (1992) Standing from left to right: Cecil Shewchuk, SACDA CEO, Eric Leaver, SACDA director, Steve Waite, SACDA operations, Susan Scott, SACDA Marketing, Stu McBride, SACDA chairman, Grant Stevenson, SACDA development Seated: Robert Maxwell, vice-president, Honeywell Canada (Photo courtesy of Sacda Ltd.)

In the early days, the enthusiasm for developing commercial enterprises at Western was muted largely because of the perceived risks. It required considerable expertise from people with industry experience, like Eric Leaver, who helped make it work and grow. Once launched, Sacda Ltd. expanded rapidly to have offices in England, Singapore, United States, and Australia, as well as in Vancouver and Montreal, Canada. Its customers hailed from all over the world. In 1993, the company won the London Chamber of Commerce's Outstanding Business Achievement Award.

SACDA was a 20-year project from its inception to the multi-million dollar business it has become within Honeywell. Fundamental to the success of the venture was the support of people of vision at Western, especially in the university administration and the Faculty of Engineering Science, patient investors, industry advisors, and the many dedicated hard-working employees along the way.

Cecil Shewchuk, faculty member and member of the Advisory Committee

Electrical Shop

I recall my very long job interview with John Watkinson, Head Technician in the Electrical Shop, which included a technical exam given by Bob Kettlewell. The thing I remember most was that after five hours of interview John commented that I didn't say much. He talked so much that I could not get a word in sideways. Afterwards I was unsure if I had enough money to pay to get out of the parking lot, as I had figured I'd be there an hour tops. It was both a strange and wonderful experience but the bottom line was that I did get the job.

John was, of course, quite a character and was well known for singing in the halls along with the custodian, Mateo, who sang classical operas in Italian. John would compete with Gilbert and Sullivan operettas. He decorated the ceiling of the shop with various model airplanes and could describe the technical specifications of each model. Also there was the time that John decided that the shop needed painting so he decided that it should be "battleship grey" – he purchased the paint then showed up on weekends to apply it.

One other event I thought was funny, if not a little daring at the time. The Computer Science and Math departments used to have space in the Spencer Building. When they moved out, there were several unoccupied rooms. John decided if no one else had plans for these rooms, possession was 9/10 of the law and he would claim them. He simply moved equipment into these rooms and I guess when people started looking around for space, they would see a room occupied and left it as is. There are a couple of rooms the electrical department is still using because John did this. It is rather unlikely anyone could pull this off now, as space is so tightly controlled and we've seen people with tape measures sizing up rooms in order to justify getting more space or to keep the space they have.

Tim Hunt, Member of the Technical Staff (Electrical Shop and Information Technology Group), 1980-present.

New Opportunity

As new immigrants to Canada, my family and I were lucky to be sent by Immigration Canada to London in January 1985. The next year I was hired as mechanical technician in the Department of Mechanical Engineering by Professor John Tarasuk.

I was lucky person because I couldn't get a job in my profession as an environmental engineer, although fortunately I had attended a mechanical technical school in my youth.

The most difficult times were the first three months at my new job when I had to learn a lot about my new duties.

The first two years were not easy, but for the next 15 years I was really happy to work in this environment alongside the very friendly professors and colleagues at our faculty. Thinking about our life in Canada and thanks to our work in Western, specifically the friendly work environment, we feel very happy and thankful to be part of the big Western family.

Marian Jaworski, technical staff member 1986-2003

Why is it called Western Ontario?

My wife Kathy and I were recruited to Western from Sydney, Australia in 1978. At the time we were considering whether to accept an offer, we decided to look on a map to find out where London was located. We pulled out a map of Ontario and since it was the University of Western Ontario, we started at the Manitoba border and started looking east. We were rather amazed at how far Western (and London) actually was geographically from western Ontario. The name still puzzles me today.

At the time I was recruited, the only person I knew was Barry Vickery, who had been a professor at the University of Sydney before he moved to Western a few years earlier. He told me how good it was in Canada (and how cheap the beer was – those were the days!). We landed at London international airport on Dec. 8, 1978 – to be met at the airport by Barry and Bob Quigley (who was head of the Geotechnical Section I was joining). Barry, however, was wearing a cast on a newly broken wrist, having slipped on the ice a few days earlier. Suddenly we became acutely aware winters in London (southern Ontario) were not like winters in Sydney. The civil group, indeed the faculty, was still small then. Mel Poucher (head of the Civil Group) invited us to meet faculty and their wives at a Christmas get-together at his home. We discovered what a friendly group we had joined. But the prime topic of conversation at the party was the snowstorm during the previous winter, which closed the university for three days and forced some people to sleep in their offices since they could not get home after the storm struck. There was no mention of this at the time of recruitment. Welcome to Canada!

Not long after I arrived, the faculty acquired a new 'powerful' computer. As a modeller, I was indeed delighted. There was an official opening to which faculty was invited and I decided to attend. After the formal ceremonies, Dean Chess came over to me and said, "Kerry, is your idea of dressing up to put on a sweater?" Then I noticed most faculty members wore a coat and tie everyday (except in summer). It was a formality I had not been used to and which remained for many years. Message received; after that I wore my coat and tie every day in the teaching terms. It had one hidden advantaged for an assistant professor in his mid-20s: visitors stopped assuming I was a graduate student.

Kerry Rowe, Civil Engineering faculty member, 1978-2000

Recollections of my time at Western

When I arrived at The University of Western Ontario that sunny September morning on the first day of classes, I already had a degree to my name in an area that groomed students for possible entry into medical school. The students were competitive, and lasting relationships were hard won. There was not much team spirit, unlike the Engineering students at the other end of the campus.

One of the things that really stood out for me during my time at Western was the sense of welcome and camaraderie. We were all on a team and in this together. There was fun and education to be had, but the journey was in many ways, going to be the reward. This sentiment was carried through not only the students, but the faculty as well. I remember, in particular, sitting in the cafeteria in the mornings, and having many faculty members, (in particular, professors Quigley, Duerden and Bonnema, among others), walk over and sit down with me before heading off to our respective classes. We would discuss life, society, the economy and many topics, not just the course material or the results of a test. They took the time to get to know me as a person and this was an extraordinary contrast to the academic environment I previously experienced. It left an impression on me that has stayed with me ever since. Bravo Faculty of Engineering, Bravo Western!

Dev R. Sainani, BESc'83, MESc'86, PhD'96

Hockey and the Wind Tunnel

Alan Davenport influenced my entire career from the beginning when Jean and I came to the inaugural wind tunnel conference in 1965, to the tragic dinner party at our house in 2009 when his ongoing battle with Parkinson's came to an end. His accomplishments are well documented, but to me it will always be the breadth of his interests, his enthusiasm and encouragement, and his incredible tolerance and love for life that made the difference.'

Hockey had always been a passion of mine, although disconnected from any significant skillset I came to as a graduate student. I introduced the idea of a wind tunnel fun hockey game early in my tenure, and although it required people to desert their posts for the best part of two hours around lunch on a working day, Alan happily supported the idea in spite of reservations in other quarters. For years, this involved almost everyone, including the female staff and the international students. Although we could never induce Alan to play, without his support it would never have lasted as it has (in a bit more serious form) to this day.

In fact, it was a successful spirit building exercise, bringing together most of the wind tunnel people and a few from other departments. I remember playing on the outdoor rink with Kevin McNamara, a student who could barely stand up on skates and was more comfortable with a hurling stick, which he used in place of a hockey stick. He managed to get to center ice and completely dominate. Beware anyone who got within range.

And there was the day many years later when we graduated to the indoor rink and were sometimes invaded by hotshots interested in a pick-up game. In the midst of a game, a newcomer arrived and did his final preparations on the bench, looking very professional with all the equipment money could buy. I proceeded to skate over to tell him to get lost, when he put his first foot on the ice. This was no professional; in fact, it was a new student who needed the equipment for his own protection, as he slowly made his way around the boards.

Hockey was a great addition to the culture and just one of the many ways Alan encouraged people to experience life as a whole.

David Surry, faculty member, Boundary Layer Wind Tunnel Laboratory, 1971-2004

Chapter 6
The Innovative Years, 1987-1999
Dean R. Mohan Mathur

In 1986, Gordon Chess announced his intention to step down as dean effective June 30, 1987, so a search committee to find a suitable replacement was formed under the chairmanship of Professor Tom Collins, Provost. It was recognized by members of the committee this was an important juncture for the faculty and this appointment was indeed a critical one. The search was international in scope and many outstanding candidates were considered, but the one who rose to the fore was Professor R. Mohan Mathur, who at that time was Head of the Department of Electrical and Computer Engineering at the University of Manitoba.

Initially, Mathur was not interested in the position. However, he agreed to a site visit and met with the recruitment committee. This visit demonstrated the potential challenges and opportunities for the deanship. He returned to campus with his family in early 1987 and later accepted the position. In July 1987 he started his tenure as dean.

Perhaps here I, (GSPC), can share a personal story about this appointment:

> In 1986 I was on the selection committee for the new dean, but I was also a previous chair of what was then known as the Electrical Group. In this position I had the privilege every year of meeting with the late Bonnie Jackson, who was the university liaison for Nortel, then in its glory days. Bonnie's function was to scout out hot prospects among new graduates to hire for

Dean R. Mohan Mathur (Photo courtesy of Beta Photos)

the company and paid annual visits to every electrical and computer science department across the country. This gave him a unique perspective on what was happening in electrical engineering education in Canada. As we met that year I turned the tables on him and indicated that we were looking for a new dean and questioned whether he had any ideas on good prospects from other universities. Without missing a beat he responded, "Dr. Mohan Mathur, head of Electrical and Computer Engineering, University of Manitoba." When I showed my ignorance in stating I did not know the gentleman, Bonnie then proceeded to describe an academic Superman who was making all sorts of innovations in curriculum, research and industrial and government collaborations. In Bonnie's view, here was an individual soon to be dean at University of Manitoba.

Armed with this information, the Selection Committee soon agreed Western President George Pedersen would contact Mohan. He telephoned to gauge his interest. I was not party to the conversation, but understand Mohan immediately informed him his level of interest was zero. He was well established at the University of Manitoba, was very happy with his career path, he loved Winnipeg, his wife Aruna had a wonderful and stimulating teaching position in the university, his two children did not wish to move and they had recently designed and built their dream home on the banks of the Red River.

Fortunately for us, Pedersen persisted. Finally Mohan, the gentleman that he is, let it be known that he was in fact shortly embarking on a visit to India, but on passing through Toronto he could visit for one day. He was not visiting Western for an interview, but to meet the committee just to put their mind at rest that he really was not interested in the position.

It was a special visit; two things happened:

The first was the fact the committee was blown away by the innovative clear thinking and insights he displayed during that meeting. Before the hour was up, everyone realized he was a special catch for Western. The second thing that happened was the seeds of interest were planted in Mohan's mind and the potential challenges presented in Engineering at Western at that time captivated his imagination. He mulled them over during his Indian visit and after his return to Winnipeg, and as a result came for a follow-up visit early in 1987 with Aruna and his children, Tinu and Shihka. Finally, the Western offer was accepted and he started as dean in July 1987. This began what turned out to be a 12-year tenure, the longest term of any dean in our history, and a period of unprecedented growth and innovation.

Once the decision was made in late spring, an announcement was featured in the London Free Press and in a letter-to-the-editor dated May 4, 1987, Peter Sturdy wrote he found it depressing to see the university appoint a non-native-born Canadian as dean. Further he went on to caution, "the implications are certainly dreary for Canadian students and their parents." It was comforting to everyone to read the contents of a reply letter from President George Pedersen and Provost Tom Collins, who found the contents of Sturdy's letter appalling and stated: "We are fortunate that, after an intense search and genuine competition involving several other first-rate Canadian educators, we were able to convince Mathur to come to Western. The institution and, and our students, are indeed fortunate."

According to Mathur, the major attraction to Western was the challenge to turnaround a relatively lesser-known faculty, in spite of its early start in a big, comprehensive, research-intensive Canadian university. Soon after his arrival he undertook a critical assessment of the strengths and weaknesses of the faculty, as he perceived them.

There was much existing strength to build on. For example it was clear a relatively large number of distinguished faculty members of international repute existed in the faculty. In addition, the existing faculty members consisted of a healthy combination of backgrounds and many were alumni of outstanding institutions, such as Oxford, Cambridge, London, Imperial College, Bristol, St. Andrews, MIT, Berkley, Purdue, Sydney, Toronto, and McGill. The distinguishing feature of the faculty's approach to engineering education was its emphasis on utilizing interdisciplinary material within the five programs, as well as adding innovative sub-specialties, such as environmental and biochemical engineering. In graduate studies and research innovation, Engineering at Western was internationally known for wind engineering, and nationally recognized for Geotechnical, Applied Electrostatics and Chemical Reactor Engineering. As well, the faculty had the Engineering Science Advisory Council of influential business leaders who were interested and ready to help.

Clearly the faculty had a lot going for it at this point in its history. However, to advance to the next stage of its development, it was clear there were a number of serious issues needing to be addressed and resolved. For example, there was a lack of recognition and commitment on the part of the senior executives of the University for engineering. Indeed, it was not recognized as a priority within the planning process. Taken in comparison with other engineering schools in the province, the financial health and budget allocated for Engineering was sub-standard and there was no recognition of the fact most successful research-intensive universities attempted to keep their budgetary allotment between Engineering programs and the Sciences more or less equal. At Western in 1987, the Faculty of Science's budget was several times larger than in Engineering. The fact Engineering was not considered a University priority is best illustrated by the Renaissance Western fundraising campaign. Of the $89 million budget, the Faculty of Engineering Science's target was set at only $1 million. As a result of this type of ongoing and continued neglect by the University administration, a feeling of pessimism and helplessness prevailed among many faculty and staff members. The faculty size, as defined by student enrolment, faculty and staff numbers, and space and laboratories – in comparison with other engineering schools across Canada – was below critical. As a result, the faculty was not attracting the best quality students.

All of this was underlined by the fact in 1987 the faculty was on a short-term accreditation and was required to be re-evaluated within three years. There was no question it was a struggle to offer five degree programs with the faculty strength of only 43 base positions and five term appointments. This number had not changed significantly in more than 20 years (See Appendix 5). Student recruitment was hindered by the fact the faculty was surrounded by engineering giants, like Waterloo, Toronto, McMaster and Queen's Universities.

Finally, most decisions for Engineering were made at the dean's level, resulting in Group chairs, as well as faculty members, feeling disempowered.

Although some of these challenges were known ahead of time, the bulk of them were not. Most critically, the possible closure or scale back of the faculty had been seriously discussed at the Board of Governors level, but it was not known to anyone other than its members. One of the first major activities of Mathur after his arrival was to call together members of recently renamed Engineering Science Advisory Committee (ESAC) for an orientation meeting. One can imagine what a surprise and shock it must have been to hear this news reported by a board member, who also happened to be an alumnus.

To many, this final revelation of possible closure would send a new incumbent back to the security of a prestigious position already in hand from the President of their previous institution. However, the challenge presented by this combination of realities proved irresistible to Mathur. In true engineering style, with what to some would appear as a series of discouraging and even insurmountable problems, he recognized these problems offered a number of opportunities for the faculty to build upon.

Mathur realized having a prominent, research-intensive, comprehensive and large university as its mother institution, there was a great scope for a turnaround and drive towards excellence. Having come from Manitoba, he saw Ontario as a prosperous province, which provided great opportunities for industry partnerships. He was particularly encouraged by the opportunity of working with the members of ESAC, who offered an influential and enthusiastic team for launching a new vision for Engineering at Western.

Difficult times in the Faculty of Engineering Science

The Engineering Science Advisory Council (ESAC), consisting of business and other leaders, was formed early in the development of the Faculty of Engineering Science. The goal was to offer advice and support to the faculty, particularly in terms of innovative programs, which would enhance the relationship between the faculty and the university, as well as the business community.

There had been a number of excellent earlier chairs of ESAC, such as Carl Kohn, Assistant Vice-President at Bell Canada and John Thompson, President of IBM Canada. (See Appendix 9 for a complete listing). In late 1987, I was fortunate to succeed John as chair of ESAC, and to learn from and work with Mohan Mathur, the new dean of the faculty.

We were all quickly impressed with his knowledge, enthusiasm and proposals for the introduction of innovative new programs, such as the modular master's in Engineering and an Industrial Internship Program. We were equally dismayed to find that the administration and Board of Governors were contemplating a number of drastic steps, including reducing the program to two years, with the final two years to be completed at another university, as well as closing the Materials Science program and drastically reducing operating funds. In fact, closure of the faculty had been discussed at the Board of Governors level. Another indication of their low regard was the faculty was not included as a priority in the then "Renaissance" fundraising program.

ESAC was determined to support the faculty and its growth. It undertook two main initiatives: a study benchmarking the faculty with other Canadian Faculties of Engineering, and further strengthening the already influential membership of ESAC.

IBM Canada and MDS (a Canadian health-care company) funded the external comparative review of Western's Faculty of Engineering Science with other Engineering faculties in Canada. Metrics such as research grants per full-time equivalent student; student/faculty ratios; operating efficiency and qualifications of staff were used to provide quantitative evidence.

The report clearly showed the faculty ranked second in all of Canada and was hidden gem in Canadian Engineering education. This provided the ammunition needed by ESAC members, such as Don Smith of Ellis Don, Peter Maurice of Canada Trust, and others to 'educate' the administrative leadership and the Board of Governors of the facts needing to be considered in planning the future of the faculty.

All of this was enabled by our belief in the strategy undertaken by Dean Mathur and his leadership team. There were a large number of formal and informal meetings held by members of ESAC with the Senate, the administration and the Board of Governors, as well as with deans of related faculties. Driven by the enthusiasm and energy of Dean Mathur, by late 1989 the Faculty of Engineering Science was being recognized for its true value across the university.

ESAC was delighted to be a small part of supporting the faculty through its comparative study and meetings with leaders at the university. The ongoing success of the faculty has proven these energies were well spent.

Ron Yamada, BESc'64, Chairman of ESAC, 1987-89

Dean Mathur "hit the ground running" and within a very short period developed a strategy he sold to the administration, which included a number of specific goals and actions. This strategy included actions on a number of fronts, with the goals of: a.) Ensuring faculty growth to achieve a critical size; b.) Restoring full accreditation to all the programs; c.) Starting a faculty-run continuing education program; d.) Adding innovative aspects in the programs, their delivery, and new activities to establish uniqueness to further differentiate the faculty from others; e.) Re-creating a culture of optimism in the faculty; and f.) Strengthening ties with Engineering alumni.

Formalizing Departmentalization

One of the lasting contributions of Dean Chess was to finalize the transition from the historical Group structure, in place from 1954, to that of a faculty with five departments. Mathur arrived on July 1, 1987 and inherited the beginning of this new organization. As a transition, he confirmed the immediate interim appointments of John Beeckmans, chair, Chemical and Biochemical Engineering, Mel Poucher, chair, Civil Engineering, Alan Webster, chair, Electrical Engineering, Jim Brown, chair, Materials Engineering and John Tarasuk, chair, Mechanical Engineering.

Shortly thereafter, Ian Duerden was appointed associate dean, Undergraduate Affairs and Kerry Rowe was named associate dean, Graduate Studies and Research. Although not formally part of the administrative structure, Hugh Peacock was reaffirmed to carry on with his enthusiastic leadership of 'Program 240,' the experiential learning program pioneered at Western under which a student would volunteer 240 hours to work in industry to solve specific engineering problems. An additional change under the new structure was converting the silver medals awarded to current students with the highest standing in their disciplines to gold medals for future students (see Appendices 6 and 7 for a complete listing of all the medal recipients).

The year 1988 was very active, as Mathur began working on his ambitious agenda. Following the transition year of interim departmental leadership, Gerry Margaritis was appointed chair, Chemical and Biochemical Engineering, and Peter Castle was appointed chair, Electrical Engineering. As well, the appointments of Poucher, Brown and Tarasuk, as chairs of Civil, Materials and Mechanical departments, respectively, were formalized for a five-year term. Since Kerry Rowe received the prestigious Steacie fellowship, in his place John Beekmans was appointed associate dean, Graduate Affairs.

In early 1988, Mathur was invited to share his vision for the future of Engineering Science with the Board of Governors. He took this opportunity to describe his views on the objective of achieving an international reputation in engineering research and education for Western. He stressed the faculty was under-resourced and funding was desperately needed to increase the number of faculty and staff members, and improve teaching laboratories. It was now very clear that Industry pays a dividend when hiring graduates with co-op experience. Therefore, Western had to find ways to integrate experiential learning in its curricula. President George Pedersen reminded the Board of Governors the faculty was smaller than many departments in other universities; however, it had highly qualified members who generated research grants above the national average. He indicated the administration was committed to strengthen engineering, but noted, "we are limited in our ability to shift resources." The president stressed the success of the proposed Research and Development Park would depend entirely on encouraging and further developing applied research.

Industrial Internship Program

Starting in 1988, the faculty decided to place a higher priority on Program 240 and initiated an innovative Industrial Internship Program (IIP). This offered an alternative to the traditional Co-op Program, but was more effective as it was voluntary and easier to implement. Representatives from participating industries selected students who applied for an IIP placement.

The program was available to students who had completed the first three years of the engineering program and therefore had a good grounding in the fundamentals. The selected students could be employed by industry for eight months, 12 months or 16 months, spanning either two consecutive study terms, one added summer term, or two added summer terms respectively. The students were paid for their work, but were required to pay a placement fee, write comprehensive IIP reports, present these for examination at the faculty and get a credit on their transcripts. Thus, this program was the first of its kind and was developed to run on total cost recovery. It soon became a very desirable alternative for both students and industrial partners.

Internship students were visited at the workplace by faculty and volunteer engineers. The program was successfully nurtured and administered initially by Hugh Peacock, followed by David Harman. Its overall success is best demonstrated by the fact it was soon copied by most engineering schools in Canada.

Faculty and Alumni Affairs

The new dean was determined to create an all-inclusive culture and to encourage camaraderie amongst members of faculty and staff. For example, unlike the earlier tradition, the Faculty Christmas Party in 1987 welcomed all members of faculty and staff members. In addition to the regularly scheduled and more formal Faculty Council meetings, all faculty and staff were invited to Town Hall-style information sessions conducted by the dean, as well as periodic out-of-town strategic planning retreats. These sessions provided valuable feedback and greatly improved communication among administrators and members of faculty and staff.

The Mathur's left their custom-built dream house behind in Winnipeg. After renting for two years in London, they moved into a newly constructed house overlooking the Thames River in 1989 and it was a copy of the home they left behind. To celebrate the move, on five consecutive Saturdays, faculty and staff members, along with their spouses, were invited for a special Indian dinner prepared by the dean and his wife Aruna.

In September 1988, a Taskforce on Alumni-Faculty Relations was formed, led by former Dean Gordon Chess. This consisted of members from both constituencies and brainstormed ways in which contact with former graduates could be improved. One outcome was charging Professor George Emmerson with starting an Alumni Newsletter; the first issue was published in 1989. Special faculty receptions were organized for Engineering alumni at each Homecoming, at which a distinguished alumnus/a received the L.S. Lauchland Engineering Alumni Medal (see Appendix 8 for a listing of past recipients). In past years this medal had been presented at a University-wide event. The medal was awarded to recognize, celebrate and honor the winner's accomplishments. Later the same evening, the dean and his wife attended dinners organized for 25 and 30-year reunions, at which they distributed special gifts from the faculty to all attendees. Linkages with engineering alumni were further reinforced by periodic communications from the dean and meetings with alumni at special gatherings organized out-of-town when Mathur was visiting places such as China, Hong Kong, U.S. and various Canadian cities.

Research and Development Park

The University started developing lands and setting up a Research and Development Park that included the previous Smallman properties together with the university lands on the northwest corner of Windermere and Western Road. This enabled Engineering to have the opportunity to further support applied university research and development in close partnership with industry. Dean Mathur was appointed to the Board of the Western Research and Development Park. The opportunity was used to emphasize the valuable economic contributions already made by the Boundary Layer Wind Tunnel, Applied Electrostatics, and Geotechnical Research Centre and to add Chemical Reactor Engineering, Biomedical Engineering and Construction Technologies as new and important contributors from the small but valuable Faculty of Engineering Science. The use of this R&D Park as an incubator for industry start-ups was emphasized as a key attribute of this new facility.

Professor Hugo deLasa (left) and Professor Maurice Bergougnou in the Chemical Reactor Engineering Laboratory, 1987 (Alan Noon/Communications and Public Affairs Collection/Western Archives, Western University).

Computing Infrastructure

Engineering used its capital resources to put state-of-the-art Ethernet cabling in the lower two floors of the Spencer Engineering Building. This was later expanded to all floors once the Applied Mathematics and Statistics Departments vacated the Engineering Building. Among the educational infrastructure desperately required at this time, the most acute need was to modernize the computing labs. For many years, the Department of Statistics, Faculty of Engineering Science and Department of Applied Mathematics jointly operated a Statistics, Engineering Science, Applied Mathematics, (SEAM) facility which used a Prime computer connected to about 40 "dumb" terminals, which by 1987 was an obsolete facility. As a result, the high priority for Engineering was to replace it with modern equipment within a year. The faculty reached out to IBM Canada and struck a partnership lasting two years. With this agreement, IBM loaned hardware and software to establish a Computer Assisted Learning Laboratory for Engineering (CALL-E) with an option to purchase the material after two years. Consequently, IBM provided 40 recently developed PS/2 model 50 microcomputers, and six PS/2 model 60 microcomputers networked to be used by junior engineering students. In return, 18 engineering professors developed new educational software in support of the undergraduate program and under the agreement IBM Canada had the option to distribute this software free of charge to other universities.

This CALL-E microcomputer laboratory was a state-of-the-art facility inaugurated on October 7, 1988. The faculty gratefully acknowledged the support of John Thompson, president, IBM Canada and an alumnus (1966) of Engineering Science at Western, for his major assistance and The University of Western Ontario for granting $190,000 though the Academic Development Fund for Engineering to purchase the equipment.

The evolution of the computing infrastructure was an essential component to the ongoing success of the faculty in both teaching and research and the transitions are perhaps best described by retired Information Technology Group Associate Director Barry Kay as follows:

"Prior to 1978 the Faculty operated an IBM 1130 computer to teach students programming. In 1978 the IBM 1130 was replaced with a Prime 400 computer that was located in room 3099 and 3100. This minicomputer was part of a shared facility called the Statistics, Engineering and Applied Math (SEAM) lab. The facility was shared by the three departments, which resided in the building at that time. There was a card reader, keypunches and Volker Craig terminals that allowed the students to login to the Prime 400. It was predominately used to instruct students in Fortran programming. In the early 1980s' the Prime 400 was upgraded to a Prime 750 system that the Business School owned and made redundant.

"The Department of Computer Science moved from Engineering to Middlesex College in the mid 1980's. In the later part of the 1980's, Statistics moved out of the building and the SEAM lab was dissolved with Engineering taking over the sole operation and management of the systems. The Prime 750 was subsequently decommissioned in 1988 by the major donation from IBM Canada and the lab became known as the Computer Assisted learning Laboratory for Engineering (CALL-E). Approximately 40 PS2 Model 50 computers were installed in room SEB 1004 and 1012. Two PS2 model 60 servers were installed in the machine room running on a Token Ring network and utilizing Novell 2.0A. These systems were the first networked laboratory computers in the faculty. A mail system called Pegasus and an Internet gateway, called Charon, were added to provided emails for student use. Many applications were added for student use, including AutoCAD and WordPerfect. Eventually the PS2's were replaced with Dell Pentium computers through the generosity of Dell. Around 1990, the IBM servers were replaced with Windows-based servers. Microsoft donated software for use by students and faculty at this time.

"By the mid 1990s' there was a requirement to remove all the co axial cable and to create a wired network of Cat 3 cable terminating to a router in the building that was owned by ITS and connected everyone to the campus backbone. This provided security for everyone, stability of the network and the ability to monitor and protect PC's in the building.

"Unix systems were introduced into the faculty in the mid 1990s'. IBM RS6000; IBM Power PC's; Silicon Graphics and eventually replaced by Sun servers and Sunblade systems that were located in room 1024 and supported by what had now become the Information Technology Group. The year 1999 was a particular challenge as it ended with the Y2K looming catastrophe close at hand. Many meetings and documentation was needed to handle the 'what if the computers fail' scenario.

They never did, and the faculty continued on through into the next century with many changes to the networks and systems as the technology continued to change and evolve."

Centre for Studies in Construction

Professor Alan G. Davenport proposed the idea of expanding the scope of his work in wind studies to a more comprehensive study of construction involving broader issues, including Social Sciences. After much preparatory work a new multi-disciplinary Centre for Studies in Construction received a final approval from the Board of Governors on January 6, 1989 and the University Senate on March 16, 1989. Faculties of Engineering Science, Social Science, Science, and Law and the National Centre for Management Research and Development (NCMRD) partnered in the Centre with Davenport as its director and Dean Mathur as chair of the management board.

Modular MEng Program

Engineering could not wait to receive funds to start a continuing education program, which would allow recent engineering graduates opportunities to re-orient and or upgrade their education on part-time basis. A new program was desperately needed to remove distance barriers and offer weekend study. Therefore, a program (commonly known as the Modular MEng program) was developed where courses were repackaged for delivery in intense modules, which could be taken as needed for academic credits and could either be applied towards an MEng degree or simply taken for self- improvement and no credit.

In its initial phase, modular courses were in the areas of environmental and manufacturing engineering, suitably supported by business courses. Concerns were raised by the university about whether the program violated government regulations by charging fees in excess of the range set by the Ontario government. The situation was clarified by breaking down the fees into two separate charges for the graduate student fees and course materials. In a separate deal, the university administration agreed to return the tuition fees collected from this program to the faculty. Thus a new, self- funding and creative dimension was added in 1989 to the engineering programs. Associate Dean John Beeckmans promoted and ran the Modular MEng program. The registration of a number of engineers from GM Diesel in the first course paved the way for the program's success. The faculty was greatly appreciative of the efforts of Bill Peel, General Manager of GM Diesel, for sponsoring a number of his engineers to initially enrol in the program. Following this success, the program developed and expanded its offerings to a number of different areas.

A few years later, the deans of engineering at McMaster, Toronto, and Waterloo Universities wanted to collectively offer a similar MEng program in an Advanced Design and Manufacturing Institute (ADMI) through Material and Manufacturing Ontario, a Centre of Excellence set up by the Ontario government. Once this group learned about the Modular MEng program, Western was invited to join the group to offer this ADMI program. The innovative thinking and leadership at Western had gained recognition and provided a blueprint for inter-university collaboration.

Student Attraction

In parallel with these activities aimed at strengthening and expanding the scope of the program, a series of important initiatives were undertaken for improving the quality of students entering the program and creating a better appreciation and demand for engineering education. For example, annual breakfast meetings were held with local science teachers and guidance counselors to equip them with accurate information about engineering, career opportunities and the special features of engineering at Western. Also, if they needed further guidance or advice, offers were made to meet with them and/or their students.

An important exercise spearheaded by Professor John Tarasuk encouraged young students to pursue higher education and consider a career in Engineering. Women engineers were in demand, but the enrolment was particularly low in Mechanical Engineering. To address this shortage, Tarasuk and a third-year female student visited more than 70 schools in the London area to discuss what engineers do and where they work.

In order to excite impressionable youngsters and encourage them to pursue science and mathematics, a Discovery Western Engineering Camp was designed and initiated at Western. During 1988-89, second-year mechanical engineering student Stephanie Wilkes was selected to start this activity, sponsored by the

Undergraduate Engineering Society (UES). During the summer of 1989 she was sent to Queen's, which ran a similar program, to study it and gain experience. Starting the summer of 1990, the UES offered Discovery Western, a weeklong series of day camps for students in Grades 5 and 6. The camp instructors were engineering students and funding was provided through corporate donations and camp fees. This was a great activity and gradually expanded to Grades 5 to 10 and included instructors traveling to schools during the months of May and June, and day camps during July and August. Special French language camps were organized for students of the French school programs.

In spite of ongoing efforts starting in the 1970's to increase the numbers of female engineering students, the percentage remained stubbornly stuck at about 10 per cent. Different disciplines were more attractive to females; in particular, Chemical Engineering was consistently higher. The ongoing challenge of attracting more female students into engineering resulted in initiatives such as organizing special open houses exclusively for female students from out-of-town schools. The students arrived in buses and engineering students conducted the entire program.

To add hands on experience a special orientation was held for first-year female students called "AutoExploration," where frosh, under the supervision of trained female mechanics had the opportunity to experience the dismantling cars and taking souvenir parts home. For graduating female engineers, a special farewell dinner (partly supported by corporate donors) was organized to give them opportunities to network and learn about the work environment from participating senior female engineers.

Around the same time, Engineering became a sponsor of prizes in school science and technology fairs. The faculty members acted as judges and established prizes of summer work in engineering laboratories to the winners of technology projects.

Lynda Shaw Tragedy

In 1990 tragedy struck the faculty with the shocking news of the death of popular student, Lynda Shaw, a third-year mechanical engineering student who was murdered near Highway 401 while returning from a visit to her family home near Brampton, Ontario. She was subsequently awarded a degree posthumously and in her memory, with the generous support of former President Carlton Williams (1967-77) and faculty friend and advisory board member Don McGeachy, an annual lecture series was started. The Lynda Shaw Memorial Distinguished Lecture has welcomed many internationally recognized personalities, such as Nuala Beck, Maurice Strong, Roberta Bondar and Bjarni Tryggvason.

The Lynda Shaw tragedy

In the spring of 1990, just a few months after the 'Montreal Massacre' of fourteen women at École Polytechnique, The University of Western Ontario experienced it's own tragedy. Lynda Shaw, a third-year Mechanical Engineering student, was brutally murdered. It was Easter Sunday and Lynda was driving back to Western from her home north of Toronto to write a final exam the next day.

Lynda was an outgoing, talented young woman, very much loved by her classmates and respected by her professors. A good student, she managed to balance her studies while taking leadership in student social activities. I personally recall her as a very good student in the classes that I taught. She organized the 'after the exams barbecue,' which was held annually at our home.

Lynda's murder shocked not only Mechanical Engineering, but also the whole university and the community. In her memory, a number of students, faculty and concerned citizens felt the need to honour Lynda. They established the Lynda Shaw Memorial Distinguished Lecture. It has become an annual memorial lecture in the Faculty of Engineering, presented by select eminent scientists, educators and industrial leaders in the university and community-at-large.

John Tarasuk, Mechanical Engineering chair, 1986-99

Student Quality

The failure rate in first year engineering at Western, like elsewhere, provincially and nationally, was close to 30 per cent, which was deemed wasteful. Failed students had to withdraw from the faculty. Failure to complete first-year studies was largely attributed to the shock of the transition from high school to the academically demanding engineering programs. Therefore, an Extended First Year Program was launched to bring this withdrawal rate close to 10 per cent. The program offered guidance to students after the fall term, encouraging them to drop courses in the spring and complete the failed and/or dropped courses in a special summer term.

The combined effect of all of these initiatives led to gradual increase in the quality of student intake and increased the percentage of female students from nine per cent (1987) to 14 per cent (national average was 15 percent) by 1992, leveling at nearly 21 per cent in 1999.

The faculty brand was reinforced through carefully produced information brochures and by creating an inclusive logo "WE" for Western Engineering. This was featured in the special gifts presented to the 25- and 30-year reunion classes at Homecoming in 1991. The computing infrastructure got a second big boost in 1989 from IBM which donated high-end graphic workstations to Engineering for design and simulation studies by senior students and researchers engaged in environmental hazards, wind engineering, geotechnical, biochemical and applied electrostatics. Another distinguished alumnus, Bill Etherington (then President of IBM Canada), was instrumental in arranging this donation.

The period between the late '80's and early '90's was once again one of great budgetary restraint both within the university system province wide and internally. The faculty took pride in achieving success in almost all the competitions for budget adjustments, such as the Program Adjustment Envelopes, the Transition, and Academic Development Funds. In 1989, responding to a Western call for cases to be made to the Quality Academic and Administrative Adjustment Fund (QUAAF), Engineering succeeded in adding $250k to its base budget resulting in four new permanent faculty positions – the first major expansion in personnel in over 20 years All of these successes, together with innovative cost recovery programs that were initiated, accelerated faculty growth.

In June 1989, all five undergraduate degree programs received full accreditation for the next six years from the Canadian Engineering Accreditation Board, demonstrating successful restructuring of the undergraduate engineering curriculum. Likewise in 1991, the Ontario Council of Graduate Studies accredited all graduate degree programs for the full term of seven years. Research activities continued to expand and during 1991 and 1992 the University Senate approved the Geotechnical Research Centre and Applied Electrostatics Research Centre in recognition of the important role they played in the research activities in the faculty. The year 1992 also marked a significant shift to a higher level in the oral presentation of the final year engineering projects (ES 400). A conference with several parallel sessions, drawing industry participants to the audience as well as judges, was organized at the Western Research and Development Park. Third-year students were encouraged to attend these sessions, as well as provide operational support. These activities provided the third-year students a better understanding of what was expected of them in the following year.

Continuing its planned approach to attract industry involvement and support towards Engineering at Western, a structural analysis competition was launched in January 1993 with the assistance of Peter Higgins, an Engineering Science alumnus and his California-based consulting firm, which provided a structural design analyzed by civil engineering students for its ultimate load bearing capacity. The actual structure was then tested in the engineering lab. The closest predictions, judged by Higgins and his associates, received awards and those surpassing Higgins' own analysis received added bonus.

This was a special period in the development of the faculty's development as the multi-pronged innovative approach and hard work resulted in an enhanced reputation, in attracting high quality students overshooting the university targets, very significantly increasing its female student enrolments, and attracting new external and internal resources. The Senior Planning Group of the university in the March 1993 report, A Reassertion of Values and a Strategy for Investment in the Future, finally recognized this outcome. There was no longer any thought at the Board level that the Faculty of Engineering Science should be closed or constrained!

By 1993, SACDA moved to a Dundas Street location and the departments of Applied Mathematics and Statistics relocated to Middlesex College, yielding the entire Spencer Engineering Building for engineering use. This space was badly needed for an expanding Faculty.

At the administrative level, Professor Tom Bonnema assumed the position Associate Dean, Undergraduate Affairs, effective July 1, 1993 and John Tarasuk was reappointed as Department Chair effective August 1, 1993 for the second term until 1998 and Alan Webster was appointed Chair Electrical Engineering effective July 1, 1993 to 1998 while Professors Poucher and Margaritis continued in their roles.

In July 1993, the Faculty of Engineering Science entered into partnership with Bell Canada as part of their University Support Program in support of Tele-communications Research and Education. This Western-based initiative demonstrated a distance education partnership with Fanshawe College in CAD/CAM design. This relationship with Bell proved to be very productive as in the following years in partnership with Electrical Engineering a Telecommunications course involving lecturers from CRTC, Northern Telecom, Bell Mobility, Stentor and Industry Canada was offered as well as having one Bell employee assigned to work with the Department of Electrical Engineering for one year to both teach and help co-ordinate the course.

Another collaborative partnership was established with Ryerson Polytechnic Institute as it was approaching an imminent university status and ready to offer accredited engineering degree programs. The partnership made it possible for selected Ryerson faculty members to become adjunct professors at Western allowing them to start participation in research, jointly supervising graduate students with faculty members in engineering at Western and become eligible for receiving research grants from NSERC. In return, Engineering at Western gained access to specially equipped Ryerson laboratories and also lecture space in which to conduct MEng Modular courses in Toronto.

Student Activities

Just like the engineering alumni, the engineering student body at Western was a great asset to the faculty and was well known throughout the campus and elsewhere for its 'spirited' participation in many activities. A special relationship was developed between students and the faculty administration in order to ensure good communication and clarify expectations. To this end, Dean Mathur held periodic meetings with student leaders and organizers of events like orientation, to ensure they were both supported and safeguarded from unwanted disciplinary penalties that might be levied by the university administrators because of ill-conceived and harmful pranks staged by engineering students. For example, in the early 1990's the students pledged to close their ill-reputed paper, The Engineer, and replaced it with a more mature Purple Arm. It took time for opinions to change for the better. On hearsay, when Martha Blackburn, head of the Blackburn Group (then the publisher of the London Free Press) lodged a complaint for the lewd behavior of engineering students, a special session was organized to distinguish between facts and perception, at which the dean invited her to speak. This was a very constructive session, which led to the building of a warm relationship with Blackburn and the community. Engineering students and campus police improved their relationship and organized friendly volleyball games.

In spite of the intensity of the engineering curriculum, many students actively participated in charitable and competitive activities, such as Shinerama, the Foot Patrol, Discovery Western, the Food Bank, and charity fundraising, such as the 24-hour Relay in support of London hospitals.

To demonstrate a wholesome image of engineers, which blends their creative and artistic talents together with their technical strengths, a number of unique initiatives were undertaken. In 1990-91 in partnership with McIntosh Art Gallery on campus, a summer project called Art and New Technologies was initiated which brought selected artists to work with engineering professors in Structural and Materials engineering. This collaboration was so successful that in 1992 the McIntosh Gallery held an Art and New Technology exhibition displaying the results. The coordinator of this project, Jan Shepherd was appointed the only artist-in-residence in Engineering in Canada. Her appointment attracted a national coverage through an article in the Globe and Mail and elsewhere, and it was pointed out that MIT in the U.S. modeled this to make similar appointments.

As a further outcome of this initiative, the first Engineering Art Show, displaying the artistic and creative talents of engineering students and faculty members, attracting nearly 60 entries, was inaugurated in1992. The art show challenged the public perception of engineers as non-imaginative "techies".

In 1992, engineering students demonstrated their commitment to the continued progress and reputation of the faculty by voluntarily making an annual contribution of $40 each to a special faculty fund dedicated to support student activities.

Student Projects

The period of late 1980's and 1990's saw an increasing use of design projects as a pedagogical tool in engineering education. One manifestation of this was the emergence of a number of national and international student design competitions such as the concrete toboggan race as well as many projects aimed at improving the design and performance of the automobile. Western students were enthusiastic competitors in many of these that including challenges involving vehicles designed for ultrahigh mileage, hybrid drive, solar powered, Formula SAE and mini-Baja.

The SunStang Project

With the encouragement of Professor John Tarasuk, a number of students from Mechanical, Electrical and Materials engineering grouped together as the Solar Team under the student leadership of Matthew Butson and undertook a major challenge: design and build a solar powered car "SunStang" to compete in the World Solar Challenge 1993. This was a grueling 10-day competition in which solar cars from around the world would race across 3,007 km in Australia much of it in the outback. In the past this World Solar Challenge had entries from high-powered manufacturers like General Motors, Honda and Toyota, and a number of universities from across the world. For the 1993 World Solar Challenge a number of Canadian universities (namely McGill, Ottawa, Queen's, Waterloo and Western)

SunStang in competition in Australia, 1993 (File photo/Faculty of Engineering Science).

entered the competition. The Solar Team spent great effort to raise the resources required for designing and producing the SunStang vehicle, including cash and gifts in-kind. Once completed, the team used the SunStang prototype to inspire local school students by hosting a High-School Solar Challenge, which used small motors powered by solar power. Solar cars from other universities' were displayed during the event on May 7, 1993. Peter Lissman, the designer of the $15 million Sunraycer, the winner of 1987 World Solar Challenge, presented the keynote address. In comparison to this vehicle the SunStang was built on a shoestring budget of about $250,000. The Minister of Science Hon. Tom Hockin distributed prizes to the winning entries in the High School Solar Challenge.

Prior to the Australian race, Western entered SunStang in the Canadian Solar Challenge in November 1993. This race helped to prove the design concepts and optimized the various systems in the vehicle. Professor John Tarasuk, the faculty advisor and strongest supporter of the project, best describes the race:

Remembering the SunStang Project

The World Solar Challenge of 1989 caught our attention when General Motors set an impressive record traveling 3,000 kilometers from Darwin to Adelaide, Australia using only solar energy. Our students took up the challenge to participate in the 1993 race.

There were many constraints in the design, construction and operation of a vehicle before it was allowed to compete. For example, seat belts, a proper braking system, signal lights and a maximum of six square meters of solar cells were all mandatory. A minimum of three wheels had to be touching the ground at all times. For safety reasons the driver must be able to exit the vehicle within a prescribed period of time. More importantly the vehicle must be stable, especially while meeting an oncoming 'road train,' which is a three trailer-truck assembly.

Development of the car for the Solar Challenge of 1993 became a fourth-year project. Our team of twelve was mainly third-year students from Mechanical Engineering and one or two students from Electrical Engineering.

By June 1993, our Solar car was named 'SunStang 93'. It resembled the 1989 GM winning vehicle. The chassis was complex and overdesigned and our drive train was sprockets and chain. To maximize the solar ray-absorbing surface, the team added two vertical panels. On one side a panel pointed upward, and on the other side the panel was pointed downward. Our calculations indicated that there was a net energy gain even though there was a slight increase in drag. This system of side panels was important during the early morning and late evening operation of the car when the sun was low.

In preparation for the October 1993 race, SunStang '93 was crated and shipped to Darwin, Australia in August. It arrived safely in time for the race. Our car passed all the qualifying tests and we were off.

After a good start, we experienced a series of mechanical and electrical problems. At one point, a half-day was spent repairing the chassis. At Alice Springs, the midway point of the race, we had to withdraw. Our only consolation was many other entries had already dropped out. We later learned most of the teams who finished the race had failed to make the distance in their first attempt. Entries came from high schools, universities and even large companies, such as Honda, so the playing field was not even.

On our return to The University of Western Ontario, the students were already planning to enter the 1996 Solar Challenge.

A graduate electrical engineer, Hany Abdel Galil, who was working on his PhD, led our 1996 challenge team. This team learned from the experiences of the previous race. For example, more efficient cells were sourced and only three wheels were used.

The driving wheel was also the electric motor. The outer hub was the rotor, so no mechanical linkage was required between a motor and the driving wheel. The chassis was integral with the shell so the weight was minimized. Considerable effort was placed in the design of the instrumentation, a telemetry system and in the quality of batteries. The entire university became aware of SunStang '96. We also had what I called 'a professional beggars team'. It included Western's president George Peterson, Dean of Engineering

Mohan Mathur, a student team member and Professor John Tarasuk, who initiated the project. Together this group raised enough funds to cover the cost of the car and the travel and racing expenses of the team. We were even sponsored by Jack Cowan, an alumnus and owner of Hungry Jack's and the KFC franchise in Australia.

The car was shipped to Adelaide, but delivered to Perth due to a shipping change. The advance team of students had the challenge of getting the car from Perth to Darwin on time. This reduced our testing and preparation time in Darwin.

We were much more competitive than in our '93 race. Regretfully, we had some small setbacks. We blew a rear tire and a team member had previously sealed the wheel assembly nuts so tight it took two hours to change a tire. Near the end of the race our telemetry system failed and we couldn't be sure of the charge in our batteries. We could not risk coming to a full stop so the car was operated at a slower speed. Queen's University passed us and as a result we came in 12th in this world-class race. We were satisfied.

In this race the daily routine is to start at 8:00 a.m. and stop at 5:00 p.m. wherever you are located. One evening we stopped by the side of the road to camp in a wide ditch for the night. In the morning when I woke and shook out my sleeping bag I realized I had slept with a tarantula. I thought as it turned to me, it said, "G-day Mate!"

John Tarasuk, faculty team leader, SunStang, 1993 and 1996

Formula SAE Competition

Another annual competition that involved many students was designing, constructing and racing a special Formula SAE car. Over the years Western's entry became increasingly sophisticated within the rules allowed in the competition with the 1997 entry being particularly professional.

Dean Mohan Mathur sits in the driver's seat of the 1997 Formula SAE car, with team leaders John Armstrong (left) and Bidhi Singh (right) (Marian Jaworski/File photo, Department of Mechanical and Materials Engineering, Western Engineering).

Integrated Manufacturing Technology Institute

A significant accomplishment for the faculty in 1994 was luring the National Research Council of Canada (NRC), Institute of Advanced Manufacturing Technology (IAMT) to the Western Research & Development Park. It all started with the knowledge that NRC was in the process of consolidating its manufacturing research. In a job posting for the position of Director General of the consolidated Institute of IAMT, it was mentioned the institute might be relocated at a manufacturing-intensive location in southwestern Ontario. The dean sensed an opportunity and called a meeting of the senior executives of the university, City of London and local manufacturers. In this meeting Mathur proposed the Western Research & Development Park as the future home of IAMT. Everyone agreed to support it and NRC was presented with a proposal for a special custom designed building for IAMT, in return for a long-term lease. After long discussions and several presentations, in June 1994 NRC selected London as the site of IAMT. The City of London and the University pledged $7.5 million to support the project. The name was changed to Integrated Manufacturing Technology Institute. The centre still exists in London, although its name and scope of research have been considerably revised.

"Superdean" reappointed

After a remarkable series of accomplishments as faculty leader, the first seven-year term for Dean Mohan Mathur came to an end in 1994. His tenure to date included accelerated progress of the faculty on several fronts, such as recognition of Engineering as a university asset; increased faculty resources during difficult financial times; full accreditations of undergraduate and graduate programs; increased space and revamped laboratories; enhanced and productive industry partnerships; stronger bonds with engineering alumni; and increased enthusiasm among students, faculty and staff members. All of which created an environment of optimism and acceleration towards growth and innovation. To express their appreciation, on April 29, 1994 the faculty and staff members organized an outstanding celebration: "Superman Superdean," honoring Dean Mohan Mathur for his distinguished services. This remarkable evening was a complete surprise to the Mathur's and included a gala dinner and a series of "roasts" and presentations expressing thanks and appreciation for his successes of the previous seven years. In the words of Mohan: "this outpouring of affection and surprise celebration was indeed the most outstanding and rewarding experience of my life." Perhaps the celebration sent a message that he was needed to continue driving the faculty towards leadership. Upon receiving a glowing review of the faculty by external experts, Mathur accepted another six-year term, following a one-year (1994-95) administrative leave to catch-up on his research front.

George Pedersen completed his term as Vice Chancellor and President of the University in June 1994 and Paul Davenport was appointed his successor. In meetings prior to instatement, Mathur had opportunities to apprise Davenport and Western's Board of Governors of the value of Engineering to the University and the hardships engineering was facing to emerge as one of the best and most innovative faculties in Canada. Davenport was sympathetic to Engineering and pledged his support.

During Dean Mathur's administrative leave in 1994-95, Barry Vickery was appointed acting dean, while maintaining his ongoing research commitments in the Boundary Layer Wind Tunnel.

Demonstrating its ongoing support of the faculty, IBM partnered with Western Engineering to unveil the IBM PC Power Series Laboratory on November 27, 1995. At this time, the older 46 computers of CALL-E were replaced by an equivalent number of Power PCs with an RS-6000 server.

Dean R. Mohan Mathur portrayed as "Superdean"
(Cartoon courtesy of Alberto De Santis).

In 1995, the Canadian Engineering Accreditation Board (CEAB) reviewed the five undergraduate programs again. This time, they granted a reduced three-year accreditation to all five on the grounds of insufficient resources, which could be extended to the full term of six years after receiving a satisfactory report the faculty has been granted adequate resources by the third year. This decision brought further pressure on the university to treat Engineering as its highest priority in resource allocation. Indeed, the university lived up to its commitment and the faculty programs were accredited for the full six years without a CEAB revisit.

Following his arrival at Western, Davenport initiated the development of a new strategic plan for the university. To ensure Engineering had a strategic plan of its own that was properly aligned with the university aspirations, a faculty planning process was initiated in August 1995. Once the Senate and the Board of Governors approved the University's Strategic Plan, Leadership in Learning, in November 1995, the Faculty Council of Engineering adopted its new Strategic Plan, Engineering Leadership into the Next Millennium, on March 6, 1996. This was a particularly important process because in 1996-97 the university system in Ontario was subjected to the most intense budgetary pressures in history. Taking into account the tuition fee increases, each university on average faced a budget reduction of 9.5 per cent. In spite of this, Engineering's budget remained unchanged, with the university exercising selectivity promulgated in Western's Strategic Plan. Whereas all other faculties were subjected to cuts ranging from 6.5 per cent to 20 per cent.

Coming to grips with the reality of a viable financial future and to ensure sustainability, after due consultations with the Department of Materials Engineering students, alumni, faculty and staff members, it was reluctantly decided by the Faculty of Engineering Science to wind down the Department of Materials Engineering and its separate degree program. However, recognizing that the knowledge of materials engineering is important, a formal option in Materials Engineering was created in the BESc Mechanical Engineering program. Thus, in 1996 the resources of Material Engineering were merged with Mechanical Engineering and the new department was renamed Department of Mechanical and Materials Engineering. John Sheasby was appointed associate chair.

Building upon the successful collaboration with Bell Canada, a further partnership with industry was initiated to develop an Advanced Communication

Engineering Centre – the first of its kind in Canada. This partnership was struck with Bell Advanced Communications and Bay Networks. President Paul Davenport signed a Memorandum of Agreement on behalf of the University in March 1996. The lab was designed to develop and test the next generation of data communications technology, particularly Asynchronous Transfer Mode (ATM), as well as to train Bell and Bay staff through the faculty's modular MEng program. Bell's contribution was $400,000, including the loan of one of its key professional staff members and Bay Networks provided state-of-the-art networking equipment.

The reputation of the faculty was enhanced by the recognitions earned by its faculty members, who received many awards of distinction, including gold medals and honorary degrees from Canada and abroad. In 1992-93 was a banner year as three faculty members were honored by being awarded honorary doctorate degrees, Alan Davenport from the University of Guelph, Milos Novak, the Czech Technical University and Kerry Rowe, University of Sydney. In 1995, Professor Maurice Bergougnou received a knighthood of France's order of Academic Palms for his many research collaborations with French colleagues and exchange students in the field of fluidization and ultrapyrolysis. In 1996, Professor Ion Inculet was awarded an Honorary Degree from Western for his outstanding contributions to research in the field of Applied Electrostatics.

Ever since the days of Dean Ab Johnson, Engineering contributed significantly to the petro-chemical industries in Sarnia. In 1996, the Department of Chemical and Biochemical Engineering teamed up with Bayer Rubber and struck a five-year collaboration partnership for research in polymer materials for which Bayer Rubber contributed $750,000 and this was matched by NSERC to create the first NSERC Industrial Chair in Engineering. Judith Puskas, a Bayer researcher, was hired to assume the chair position. This partnership created a new Macromolecular Research Centre, raising the number of formal research centres and activities within the faculty to nine. These Western centres were all characterized by having a strong component of multidisciplinary activities where the team efforts of researchers flourished in a formalized structure.

At this time the centres included: the Boundary Layer Wind Tunnel Laboratory; Geotechnical Research Centre; Applied Electrostatics Research Centre; Chemical Reactor Engineering Centre; Centre for Studies in Construction; Tribology Research Centre; Macromolecular Research Centre; Institute for Catastrophic

Loss Reduction (ICLR); and the Biomedical Engineering Program. ICLR was a result of the initiative led by Alan Davenport in partnership with Canada's property and casualty insurance industry, which gifted $1 million to establish two chairs, one in Civil Engineering (Slobodan Simonovic) and the second in the Department of Geography (Gordon McBean).

Curriculum Developments: Integrated Engineering and Concurrent Degrees

A significant innovation occurred in September 1998 when the faculty introduced a new undergraduate program called "Integrated Engineering", which was the first in Canada. Professor John Beeckmans proposed the program and developed the case for it. He carried out an extensive survey of several hundred companies (mostly in Ontario) and determined what curriculum demands were the most desired. The program was designed to provide a general engineering education most suitable for smaller industries, particularly manufacturing. More than 30 years after Dean Dillon first proposed a new generalist stream in engineering science his idea came to fruition. Soon after, the University of British Columbia followed Western's lead and introduced its own Integrated Engineering program.

In this same year, the four departments in Engineering were renamed to reflect the major components of engineering offered by each. The new names became: Department of Chemical and Biochemical Engineering, Department of Civil and Environmental Engineering, Department of Electrical and Computer Engineering and Department of Mechanical and Materials Engineering.

Dual Degrees

For many years the Faculty of Engineering Science encouraged collaborative partnerships with other faculties at Western. As early as the late 1970's, students were counseled about the possibilities of undertaking a joint degree program. These opportunities meant they could be cross-credited for certain courses and stay for an extra year to earn a double degree in engineering and another subject. However, this often arose out of convenience, in cases such as a student failing a course and needing to make it up in a subsequent year. With careful planning of elective courses taken during this 'extra' year, it could lead to a second degree in other subjects. Economics was a particularly attractive option. In other cases, electrical engineering and computer science for example, it was recognized that students often had common interests and it was mutually beneficial to each discipline to plan their offerings to actively encourage joint degrees. However, it was not until 1996 when Maciej Floryan became associate dean (academic) that this program was formalized and actively encouraged and promoted. Floryan recognized many very bright students often had overlapping interests and would jump at the chance to enter a program that enabled them to earn a double degree as part of an undergraduate curriculum.

As a result Engineering introduced and formalized an innovative concurrent studies program, whereby students could earn two separate degrees from two separate faculties, but in a significantly shorter time as compared to that required for sequential studies. For example, in five years a student could earn a BESc in Engineering Science and the second degree in subjects such as business, computer science, economics or music. In six years, a student could complete degrees in engineering and law and in seven years a student could complete BESc and MD degrees. The engineering and medicine combination was unique in Canada. Since these combinations offered options and flexibility, they attracted some of the best students from throughout Canada to Engineering at Western. By 1999, about 15% of Western Engineering's undergraduate students were registered in such programs. Several other universities followed Western's lead by imitating the innovative dual degree program.

City of London Design Competition

Also in 1996, through the special efforts made by Kerry Rowe and David Harman, the Department of Civil Engineering established a unique partnership with the City of London called the City of London Design Competition.

City engineers planning a structural project shared its details with civil engineering students, under the supervision of professors, and teams of students created several competing design options and submitted these to the city. The city judged these entries and rewarded the best and most practical design. The selected designs were made available to professional consultants for further review and comment. This was an extraordinary opportunity for the students and all parties benefited from the outcome. The first such design was a pedestrian bridge constructed in 1998 at Gibbons Park across the Thames River. These competitions have continued since then, leading to a number of other successful student-designed projects.

Biomedical Engineering

Since the early 1980's, the potential for introducing a Biomedical Engineering Program at Western was recognized as a great opportunity and it had remained a high priority for the faculty. Unfortunately, the faculty was unable to fully support its existing programs' survival in a period of very tight fiscal restraint. Nonetheless, the faculty did not let this opportunity slip past its sight, particularly when hiring faculty members who had backgrounds in engineering and medical biophysics. As well, through the cross appointment of Aaron Fenster (in the Department of Electrical and Computer Engineering of Engineering Science and the Schulich School of Medicine and Dentistry), new links with the Robarts Research Institute were established. Fenster was director of a team of world-class researchers in imaging at Robarts.

To further augment engineering strength in biomedical engineering, a partnership was founded between the orthopedic surgical unit at St. Joseph's Hospital, which shared a joint appointment of Dr. Jim Johnson in Mechanical and Materials Engineering. Also, Wankei Wan, who was originally hired in Materials Engineering, was transferred to Chemical and Biochemical engineering and broadened his research to biomaterials. Thus, a partnership among researchers from Engineering, Medical Biophysics, Robarts Research Institute and St. Joseph's Hospital created a nucleus for Biomedical Engineering research and graduate studies.

Under the joint leadership and commitment of Aaron Fenster and Dean Mohan Mathur, the faculty made a funding application to the Whitaker Foundation in U.S. On the third attempt, the faculty was successful in receiving a Whitaker grant in 1998. This provided $1.4 million for Biomedical Engineering research and infrastructure development. The Biomedical Engineering group was further augmented by to include Rajni Patel, who was hired as chair of the Department of Electrical and Computer Engineering and who specialized in control and robotics. This marked the beginning of the Biomedical Engineering Program at Western, which offered specialization in imaging, biomaterials, biomechanics, and robotics. The robotics activity has become an important ingredient in the world-class organization, Canadian Surgical Technologies and Advanced Robotics Centre (C-STAR). C-STAR is a partnership of four institutions dedicated to education and research on minimally invasive robotic surgery. Patel is the director of engineering at C-STAR.

Curriculum Expansion

Around this same time the Government of Ontario was convinced by the Canadian Communication industry, particularly NORTEL Networks, to take special steps to educate and train high quality engineers specializing in the application of information technology. In response, Premier Mike Harris introduced a program called "Access to Opportunities Program," aimed at introducing new programs in universities and colleges. This proved to be a golden opportunity for the Faculty of Engineering Science. In 1998, Dean Mathur filed an application for funds to strengthen and introduce new programs in Computer and Software Engineering and increase the number of graduate students. This included the ambitious request for additional funding to bring the full-time equivalent of faculty members to 128 and invest in infrastructure. With the application's success, the program provided targeted base funding for the faculty to introduce these new programs. It also allowed for enrolment in the second year of Electrical and Computer Engineering to be gradually raised from 60 to 180 students, placing 60 students each in electrical, computer and software engineering BESc programs. This investment also resulted in extra budgetary funds for graduate studies, allowing for an increase of 60 master's and 70 doctoral students.

By 1998, the introduction of several new BESc degree programs in engineering increased the number of accredited programs to seven, namely Chemical and Biochemical, Civil and Environmental, Computer, Electrical, Integrated, Mechanical and Software engineering.

The required resources to bring the faculty above critical mass necessitated a gradual increase in the first-year enrolment target. For 1999-2000, the first-year target was 500. This had been gradually raised from 275 in 1987-88. In 1998-99, 406 students were admitted (although the target was 375). These increases placed significant strain on the teaching, research and office space in the faculty. A case for a new building was integrated into the new Campus Master Plan and involved replacing the long standing but temporary building, originally built to house the Wind Tunnel and Bioengineering and now housing Chemical and Biochemical Engineering, with a larger space. In the interim, subsequent to the move of Library Science, engineering was provided with new renovated space for offices, laboratories and classrooms across Western Road at Elborn College. (Following the completion of the Thompson Engineering Building in 2003, the Departments of Chemical and Biochemical Engineering and Electrical and Computer Engineering, and the University Machine Shop, moved into the new building.)

After 12 years in office, Dean Mathur announced he wished to take an early retirement to take up a new challenge as vice-president in the Nuclear Division of Ontario Power Generation beginning September 1, 1999. Professor Ian Moore was appointed acting dean for the period September 1999 until June 2000. Thus ended a period of unprecedented expansion and success for the faculty and Mathur left the institution in a strong position to face the challenges of the new millennium.

Memories from the Mathur era

'Polar Stick' Bridge Competition

One year Mike Naish and I, as Mechanical students, decided to try to beat the Civil students in their famous Polar Stick Bridge Competition. We spent days researching and designing the best bridge to ever come from the university student population. We stayed up all night before the day of the competition gluing polar sticks to bring our design to life. The next morning, we proudly carried our bridge into the competition hall. One after another, the Civil bridges failed with loud cracks of snapping wood. It was our turn, and with the first weight applied, our bridge slowly, but surely, sank into a pile of polar sticks and wet glue on the floor below. We had forgotten one crucial element in our strategy and that was to allow enough time for the glue to dry! Needless to say, we quietly sneaked out of the competition hall, never to show our faces again in a Civil bridge building competition.

Scott Shawyer, BESc'96

Finding answers to difficult questions

"...And the solution should be obvious" grumbled the professor through a thick Russian accent as he left the derivation incomplete and made a quick exit from our first year calculus class. But very little was obvious in those early days.

Everything was novel, exciting and challenging. Most moments were spent stretching in new ways. Whether figuring out how to increase the load on a Polar Stick Bridge, how to transport 1,000+ students to a pig roast, or how to (re)launch the Purple Arm engineering student newspaper.

The best memories of Western Engineering involved important questions like these: Questions where the solution was not obvious.

Dylan Hardy, BESc'99 (Chemical)

A Touch of Class: Civil 1990

Looking back a quarter century ago at our days on Western Engineering Campus, we can't help but think of all the laughs, stories, assignments, exams, friendships, and bonds we made over four stressful years of our lives studying engineering. Well...that's for those of us that completed our degrees in four years!

Our Civil Class of 1990 was a small, united bunch outnumbered by our mechanical and electrical colleagues by a ratio of almost seven to one. But that didn't faze us, as we boasted having three female classmates, which accounted for one third of total female students that class year.

Be it through sports, doing labs, hitting the books, or socializing, the bonds of friendship created during those four years were forged stronger than Ian Duerden's ductile steel, Harmer's wood beam, Lo's bedrock, Poucher's concrete, and Peacock's structural steel all combined and tested in Surrey's water flume and Davenport's wind tunnel. Our class trips to see Nanticoke's steel mill and the Dominion Bridge in Toronto, along with the annual concrete toboggan races in Whistler and Calgary, made for some great sightseeing and memories. At Whistler, our concrete toboggan boasted one of the shortest stopping distances in spite of the fact our combined team and sled weight barely had us flying over 25 km/hr

159

down a steep hill. Proudly named the 'Mustang Mercedes,' we modified a Mason jar lid with a gold plastic cutout for our emblem.

Since walking out of those Western doors in 1990 with our hard-earned degrees in hand, we've still managed to reunite and turn back the hands of time to reminisce about these and many other stories every five years, alongside some dedicated mechanical/electrical diehards we've adopted as part of our class.

Thanks to all the deans, professors, secretaries, and grad students who helped us along the way. We're forever grateful for the education and thanks for the memories!

From the Civil'90 Class and Beyond: Leonard, Rob B., Kevin, Rob D., Antony, Sergio, Dean, Colleen, Sean, Blaik, Sharon, Mike, Scott, Mark, Mike, Matt, Rick, Lucia and Bassim, along with our adopted Mechs/Chems/Elects: Jas, Ed, Henry, Steve, Peter and many others I'm sure I'm missing.

Robert Bressan, Civil'90 Class representative

Finding off-road adventure

The Mini Baja is an off-road vehicle that is designed and built to participate in an annual international student design competition, which is sanctioned by the Society of Automotive Engineers (SAE). The Western Mini Baja team was formed in the late 1990s and the first vehicle to participate in the competition was in Orlando, Florida in 1999. The team managed to raise enough funds to construct a vehicle, but had little leftover for the logistics of participating in the event. However, with determination they managed to obtain some funds from the faculty of Engineering Science and convinced the Physical Plant department to loan them a van, which operated on propane fuel. We thought this was a great bonus as propane fuel was cheaper than gasoline. However, little did we know the inconvenience and added expense this involved.

The unfortunate thing was the vehicle was outfitted with a small propane storage tank, as it was only intended for use around the university. In addition, the use of propane fuel for operating vehicles in the U.S. is not as common as in Canada; therefore it was very difficult to find a place to buy propane fuel. The team quickly figured out that Flying J Truck Stops and KOA Campgrounds were the place to go to get propane fuel. There were many times along the way where the distance between Flying J Truck Stops was too great and we were forced to drive to a KOA Campground, which typically was over half-hour off the main route. It was all worth it as the team had a great experience and they managed to bring home a third place trophy in the suspension and traction event.

The 1999 Western Mini Baja team at the competition site in Florida.
Team members from left to right are: Dave Lunn, Michael Jenkins,
Scott Calnek and David Lee (Photo courtesy of Dave Lunn).

Dave Lunn, BESc'01, Mechanical and Materials Engineering technical staff member, 1994-present)

Candy, Moon Dust and the "Vomit Comet"

During my 33 years in working in the mechanical shop much of my time was spent dedicated to work in the Applied Electrostatics Research Centre working on projects supervised by Professor Inculet. Although trained as a toolmaker, I soon became skilled in handling high voltage power supplies safely. There was never an opportunity to become bored as the variety of the applications ranged over many applications from electrostatic pesticide spraying, to an electrostatic vacuum cleaner, and it is hard to remember them all.

Three particular projects do stand out: One involved developing an electrostatic technique to improve the manufacture of a popular candy brand by improving the uniformity of the thin layer of sugar that covers the chocolate core before the outside coloured layer is applied. In order to test this, I constructed a test bed involving a rotating drum about 18 inches diameter and 10 feet long. During each test more than 100lbs or so of chocolate pellets was fed through the system. As a large number of tests were required, word quickly spread in the faculty that containers of hundreds of pounds of chocolate cores were arriving in the laboratory. Naturally, not all of the chocolate was required for the tests with the result that there was no lack of takers within the ranks of staff, faculty and students to ensure that none of the surplus went rancid with the result that everyone's sweet tooth was satisfied.

During the period following the Apollo missions a lot of effort was expended in trying to find ways to separate the valuable minerals in the dust found on the surface of the moon. Electrostatic separation proved to be particularly attractive because the moon's atmosphere is a vacuum and the gravity is 1/6 that of the Earth. We carried out tests in the laboratory on simulated moon dust and following promising results Professor Inculet was invited to visit the NASA repository to view the actual samples returned from the moon. He reported this was a huge clean room protected like Fort Knox.

In the 90s, Professors Inculet and Floryan won a contract from the Canadian Space Agency to study the behavior of water droplets exposed to an electric field in zero gravity conditions. This involved the construction a very elaborate self-contained chamber that would perform and record the experiment automatically during the brief 30 seconds or so of zero gravity that occurred when a NASA plane performed a series of parabolic arcs. Along with a graduate student and Professor Floryan and a NASA technician, I accompanied this experiment in the plane on four separate flights. Although I myself only ever felt queasy we soon discovered why this continual acceleration and deceleration caused these flights to be known quite accurately as the "vomit comet."

Dave Woytowich, technical staff member, 1967-2000

Chapter 7
Enter the New Millennium

Here is where this part of the history of Engineering Science at Western stops for now. Certainly not because there is nothing more to report but, as stated in the preface, it was felt more time needs to pass before the story should be extended. The Faculty owes much to the past deans and chairs who led the advances from the beginning in 1954 through the latter part of the 20th century (see Appendix 10 for a complete listing). In addition, all the staff and students who contributed so much and can be credited with helping to establish Western Engineering as a major player in Canada in engineering education and research.

Clearly much has happened between 1999 and 2014. For a start, in spite of great apprehensions about the potential fallouts from the threat to computing infrastructure as a result of Y2K (the year 2000), there was no interruption in the upward trajectory established during the deanship of Mohan Mathur. Under the capable leadership of acting Dean Ian Moore, a smooth transition occurred with the appointment of Dean Franco Berruti, who held office from 2000 to December 2007. Acting Dean George Knopf guided the faculty until the arrival of Dean Andrew Hrymak in July 2009. At the time of writing, Hrymak just completed one very successful term and has been re-appointed until 2019. Other than Ian Moore, who is currently at Queen's University, all of these are still very active in the faculty and contributing immensely to its ongoing successes and continuing innovations. As such, it is premature to relegate them to a history story.

These two most recent eras have seen many ongoing activities and major capital developments that include the construction of two new engineering buildings on campus: the Thompson Engineering Building (2003) and the Claudette MacKay- Lassonde

Pavilion (2009). In addition, there has been significant expansion in both the number of personnel and programs. Particularly exciting has been the further movement of the faculty's research presence into the industrial community with three off campus initiatives that have grown out of faculty strength in wind engineering, chemical reactor engineering and materials science. These include the Wind Engineering, Energy and Environment (WindEEE) Dome, the world's first hexagonal wind tunnel, the Institute for Chemicals and Fuels from Alternative Resources (ICFAR), which is devoted to advanced research in green energy sources, and the Fraunhofer Project Center for Composites Research at Western, the first major collaboration between the German-based Fraunhofer Institute and a Canadian university.

When President G. Edward Hall initiated the move to establish an engineering presence at Western, he visualized an optimum complement of 4,000 students. Today Western has almost 37,000 students, of which about 2,000 are in engineering. Comparing the campus aerial photo below with that shown in Chapter 1, it is hard to imagine how anyone could have predicted such extraordinary expansion.

Aerial view of the campus of The University of Western Ontario,
looking north, summer 2001, note there are no golf greens in sight
(Alan Noon/Western Archives, Western University).

So to conclude this story for now, just as I have taken the liberty of building upon the document produced by George Emmerson in 1979, it is hoped that at an appropriate time in the future someone else will be moved to continue the story up to 2014 – the 60th anniversary of the start of engineering at Western and beyond.

Appendix 1:
Number of BESc Degrees by Year and Discipline

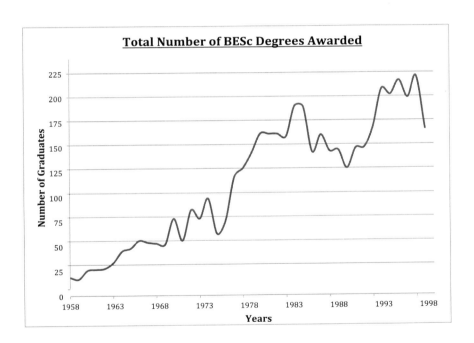

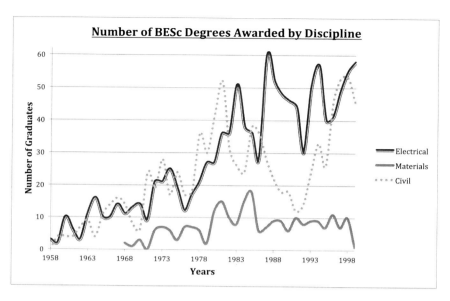

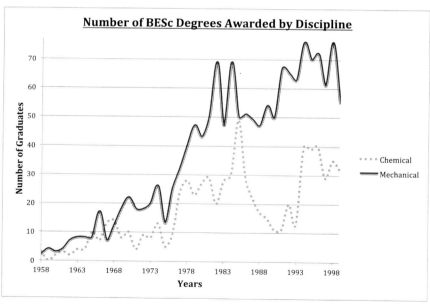

168

Appendix 2:
Full-Time Student Enrolment By Year

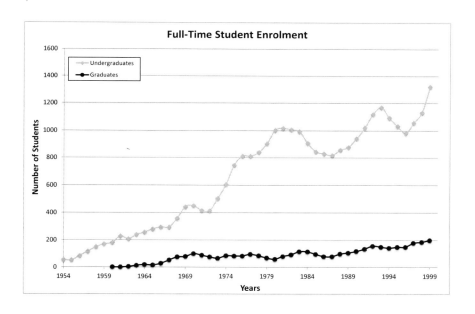

Appendix 3:
Number of Graduate Degrees By Year

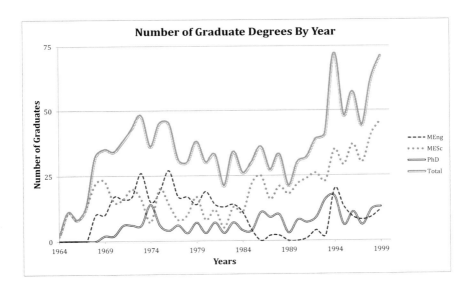

171

Appendix 4:
Number of Full-Time Faculty Members By Year

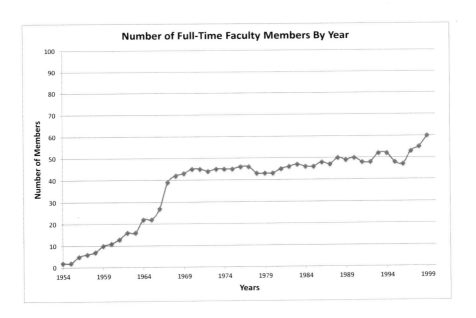

Appendix 5:
Members of Faculty During Deanship Transition Years

It is not feasible to properly recognize all the faculty and staff who have served over the 45 year period of this history. What follows is a listing of faculty as shown in the university calendar for the transition years between each of the deanships. Unfortunately, it was not feasible to do the same for staff as appropriate records are not available.

Departments of Engineering Science
University College
1959-1960

Department Faculty Members

Chairman, Lauchland, L. S., Professor, *Electrical*

Bulani, W., assistant professor, *Chemical*
Chess, G.F., lecturer, *Electrical*
Davis, W.H., lecturer, *Civil*
Emmerson, G.S., associate professor, *Mechanical*
Foreman, J.E.K., associate professor, *Mechanical*
Kearns, J.L., associate professor, *Chemical*
Olson, A.T., assistant professor, *Mechanical*
Poucher, M.P., assistant professor, *Civil*
Stewart, J.W., assistant professor, *Mechanical*

Faculty of Engineering Science
1971-1972

Officers of Administration

Dean: R.M. Dillon
Administrative Officer: J.J. Miller
Secretary of the faculty: W.H. Davis
Student Services Officer: W.H. Peacock
Group Chairmen:
Chemical and Biochemical Engineering: J.E. Zajic
Civil Engineering: M.P. Poucher
Electrical Engineering: I.I. Inculet
Materials Science: J.D. Brown
Mechanical Engineering: J.E.K. Foreman
Core Studies: G.S. Emmerson

Members of Faculty

S.H. Abu Sitta, associate professor, *Civil*
C.G.J. Baker, assistant professor, *Chemical and Biochemical*
T.E. Base, assistant professor, *Mechanical*
J.M. Beeckmans, associate professor, *Chemical and Biochemical*
*E.A. Beecroft, professor, *Political Science*
M.A. Bergougnou, associate professor, *Chemical and Biochemical*
T. Bonnema, assistant professor, *Electrical*
J.D. Brown, associate professor, *Materials Science*
W. Bulani, professor, *Chemical and Biochemical*
G.S.P. Castle, assistant professor, *Electrical*
G.F. Chess, associate professor, *Electrical*
W.H. Davis, associate professor, *Civil*
S.M. Dickinson, assistant professor, *Mechanical*
R.M. Dillon, associate professor, *Civil*
A.G. Davenport, professor, *Civil*

I.J. Duerden, assistant professor, *Materials Science*
G.S. Emmerson, associate professor, *Mechanical*
J.E.K. Foreman, professor, *Mechanical*
A.J. Frick, assistant professor, *Civil*
G.A. Geach, professor, *Material Science*
I.I. Inculet, professor, *Electrical*
N. Isyumov, assistant professor, *Civil*
G.T. Knights, assistant professor, *Civil*
N. Kosaric, assistant professor, *Chemical and Biochemical*
L.S. Lauchland, professor, *Electrical*
C.E. Livingstone, assistant professor, *Electrical*
K.Y. Lo, associate professor, *Civil*
J.A. MacDonald, assistant professor, *Mechanical*
A.M. MacKenzie, lecturer, *Civil*
M. Novak, associate professor, *Civil*
E.S. Nowak, professor, *Mechanical*
A.T. Olson, associate professor, *Mechanical*
W.H. Peacock, assistant professor, *Civil*
M.P. Poucher, professor, *Civil*
R.M. Quigley, professor, *Civil*
P.A. Rosati, assistant professor, *Civil*
C. Roy, associate professor, *Materials Science*
J.S. Sheasby, assistant professor, *Materials Science*
K.A. Sheistad, associate professor, *Chemical and Biochemical*
*M.H. Sherebrin, assistant professor, *Biophysics*
J.W. Stewart, associate professor, *Mechanical*
*P.J. Sullivan, assistant professor, *Applied Math*
W.Y. Svrcek, assistant professor, *Chemical and Biochemical*
R.K. Swartman, associate professor, *Mechanical*
J.D. Tarasuk, assistant professor, *Mechanical*
V. Vitols, assistant professor, *Chemical and Biochemical*
*P.O. Wilkins, assistant professor, *Bacteriology*
J.E. Zajic, professor, *Chemical and Biochemical*

* Joint Appointments

Faculty of Engineering Science
1977-1978

Officers of Administration

Dean: A.I. Johnson
Associate Dean: G.F. Chess
Group Chairmen:
Chemical and Biochemical Engineering: J.M. Beeckmans
Civil Engineering: A.G. Davenport
Electrical Engineering: G.F. Chess
Materials Science: J.S. Sheasby
Mechanical Engineering: A.T. Olson
Core Studies: J.D. Tarasuk

Members of Faculty

C.G.J. Baker, associate professor, *Chemical and Biochemical*

T.E. Base, assistant professor, *Mechanical*

J.M. Beeckmans, professor, *Chemical and Biochemical*

L.A. Behie, assistant professor, *Chemical and Biochemical*

M.A. Bergougnou, professor, *Chemical and Biochemical*

T. Bonnema, associate professor, *Electrical*

J.D. Brown, associate professor, *Materials Science*

W. Bulani, professor, *Chemical and Biochemical*

G.S.P. Castle, associate professor, *Electrical*

G.F. Chess, professor, *Electrical*

A.G. Davenport, professor, *Civil*

W.H. Davis, associate professor, *Civil*

S.M. Dickinson, assistant professor, *Mechanical*

I.J. Duerden, associate professor, *Materials Science*

G.S. Emmerson, professor, *Mechanical*

J.E. Foreman, professor, *Mechanical*

G.A. Geach, professor, *Materials Science*

D.J. Harman, assistant professor, *Civil*

I.I. Inculet, professor, *Electrical*

N. Isyumov, assistant professor, *Civil*

A.I. Johnson, professor, *Chemical and Biochemical*

N. Kosaric, associate professor, *Chemical and Biochemical*

Z. Kucerovsky, assistant professor, *Electrical*

L.S. Lauchland, professor emeritus, *Electrical*

K.Y. Lo, professor, *Civil*

J.A. MacDonald, associate professor, *Mechanical*

J.W. MacDougall, assistant professor, *Electrical*

A. Margaritis, assistant professor, *Chemical and Biochemical*

G.D. Moan, assistant professor, *Materials Science*

M. Novak, professor, *Civil*

E.S. Nowak, professor, *Mechanical*

A.T. Olson, associate professor, *Mechanical*

W.H. Peacock, associate professor, *Civil*

M.P. Poucher, professor, *Civil*

R.M. Quigley, professor, *Civil*

P.A. Rosati, associate professor, *Civil*

J.S. Sheasby, professor, *Materials Science*

K.A. Shelstad, associate professor, *Chemical and Biochemical*

M.H. Sherebrin, honorary lecturer, *Electrical*

C.F. Shewchuk, assistant professor, *Chemical and Biochemical*

J.W. Stewart, associate professor, *Mechanical*

P.J. Sullivan, associate professor, *Applied Math*

J.L. Sullivan, professor, *Chemical and Biochemical*

R.K. Swartman, associate professor, *Mechanical*

J.D. Tarasuk, associate professor, *Mechanical*

B.J. Vickery, associate professor, *Civil*

A. Watson, assistant professor, *Electrical*

A.R. Webster, assistant professor, *Electrical*

J.E. Zajic, professor, *Chemical and Biochemical*

Faculty of Engineering Science
1987-1988

Officers of Administration

Dean: G.F. Chess
Associate Dean: T. Bonnema
Group Chairmen:
    Chemical and Biochemical Engineering: J.M. Beeckmans
    Civil Engineering: M.P. Poucher
    Electrical Engineering: A.R. Webster
    Materials Science: J.S. Sheasby
    Mechanical Engineering: J.D. Tarasuk

Members of Faculty

R.E. Baddour, associate professor, *Civil*

T.E. Base, professor, *Mechanical*

J.M. Beeckmans, professor, *Chemical and Biochemical*

M.A. Bergougnou, professor, *Chemical and Biochemical*

C.L. Briens, assistant professor, *Chemical and Biochemical*

J.D. Brown, professor, *Materials Science*

W. Bulani, professor, *Chemical and Biochemical*

G.S.P. Castle, professor, *Electrical*

G.F. Chess, professor, *Electrical*

A.G. Davenport, professor, *Civil*

W.H. Davis, associate professor, *Civil*

H. De Lasa, associate professor, *Chemical and Biochemical*

S.M. Dickinson, professor, *Mechanical* J.R. Dickinson, associate professor, *Electrical*

J.R. Dryden, assistant professor, *Materials Science*

I.J. Duerden, associate professor, *Materials Science*

J.M. Floryan, assistant professor, *Mechanical*

J.E.K. Foreman, professor, *Mechanical*

W.D. Greason, assistant professor, *Electrical*

D.J. Harman, associate professor, *Civil*

N. Isyumov, associate professor, *Civil*

N. Kosaric, professor, *Chemical and Biochemical*

Z. Kucerovsky, associate professor, *Electrical*

K.Y. Lo, professor, *Civil*

J.A. MacDonald, associate professor, *Mechanical*

J.W. MacDougall, associate professor, *Electrical*

A. Margaritis, professor, *Chemical and Biochemical*

M. Novak, professor, *Civil*

E.S. Nowak, professor, *Mechanical*

A.T. Olson, associate professor, *Mechanical*

W.H. Peacock, associate professor, *Civil*

M.P. Poucher, professor, *Civil*

R.M. Quigley, professor, *Civil/ Geology*

I. Reid, assistant professor, *Materials Science*

P.A. Rosati, associate professor, *Civil*

R.K. Rowe, professor, *Civil*

J.S. Sheasby, professor, *Materials Science*

K.A. Shelstad, associate professor, *Chemical and Biochemical*

D.M. Shinozaki, associate professor, *Materials Science*

A.V. Singh, assistant professor, *Mechanical*

D. Surry, associate professor, *Civil*

J.D. Tarasuk, professor, *Mechanical*

B.J. Vickery, professor, *Civil*

A.R. Webster, professor, *Electrical/Physics*

G.S. Emmerson, professor emeritus, *Mechanical*

G.A. Geach, professor emeritus, *Materials Science*

L.S. Lauchland, professor emeritus, *Electrical*

J.W. Stewart, professor emeritus, *Mechanical*

J.L. Sullivan, professor emeritus, *Chemical and Biochemical*

Faculty of Engineering Science
1999-2000

Officers of Administration

Dean: R.M. Mathur
Associate Dean: J.M. Floryan
Department Chairmen:
Chemical and Biochemical Engineering: A. Margaritis
Civil and Environmental Engineering: R.K. Rowe
Electrical and Computer Engineering: A.R. Webster
Mechanical and Materials Engineering: J.D. Tarasuk

Members of Faculty

K. Adamiak, associate professor, *Electrical*
R.E. Baddour, professor, *Civil*
F.M.P. Bartlett, assistant professor, *Civil*
T.E. Base, professor, *Mechanical*
A. Bassi, assistant professor, *Chemical and Biochemical*
J.M. Beeckmans, professor, *Chemical and Biochemical*
T. Bonnema, associate professor, *Electrical*
C.L. Briens, professor, *Chemical and Biochemical*
R.O. Buchal, assistant professor, *Mechanical*
G.S.P. Castle, professor, *Electrical*
H.I. De Lasa, professor, *Chemical*
J.R. Dryden, associate professor, *Materials Science*
R.A. Eagleson, assistant professor, *Electrical*
A. El Damatty, assistant professor, *Civil*
M.H. El Naggar, assistant professor, *Civil*
J.M. Floryan, professor, *Mechanical*
W.D. Greason, professor, *Electrical*
A. Hafid, assistant professor, *Electrical*
H.M. Hangan, assistant professor, *Civil*

D.J. Harman, associate professor, *Civil*

I.I. Inculet, professor, *Electrical*

N. Isyumov, professor, *Civil*

J. Jiang, associate professor, *Electrical*

J.A. Johnson, assistant professor, *Mechanical*

A. Jutan, professor, *Chemical and Biochemical*

D.G. Karamanev, assistant professor, *Chemical*

R.E. Khayat, associate professor, *Mechanical*

G.K. Knopf, associate professor, *Mechanical*

G. Kopp, assistant professor, *Civil*

Z. Kucerovsky, professor, *Electrical*

J. LoVetri, associate professor, *Electrical*

J.W. MacDougall, associate professor, *Electrical*

D. Makrakis, assistant professor, *Electrical and Computer*

A. Margaritis, professor, *Chemical and Biochemical*

R. Martinuzzi, associate professor, *Mechanical*

R.M. Mathur, professor, *Electrical*

C.K. Mechefske, assistant professor, *Mechanical*

I.D. Moore, professor, *Civil*

R.V. Patel, professor, *Electrical and Computer*

S.L. Primak, lecturer, *Electrical*

J. Puskas, professor, *Chemical and Biochemical*

P.A. Rosati, professor, *Civil*

R.K. Rowe, professor, *Civil*

J.Q. Shang, assistant professor, *Civil*

J.S. Sheasby, professor, *Materials Science*

J.L. Shen, assistant professor, *Mechanical*

D.M. Shinozaki, professor, *Materials Science*

A.V. Singh, associate professor, *Mechanical*

A.G. Straatman, assistant professor, *Mechanical*

D. Surry, professor, *Civil*

J.D. Tarasuk, professor, *Mechanical*

W.K. Wan, associate professor, *Materials Science*

A.R. Webster, professor, *Electrical and Physics*

E. Yanful, associate professor, *Civil*

C. Zhang, associate professor, *Mechanical & Mats Sci*

J. Zhu, associate professor, *Chemical and Biochemical*

M.A. Bergougnou, professor emeritus, *Chemical and Biochemical*

J.D. Brown, professor emeritus, *Materials Science*

W. Bulani, professor emeritus, *Chemical and Biochemical*

G.F.H. Chess, professor emeritus, *Electrical*

A.G. Davenport, professor emeritus, *Civil*

W.H. Davis, professor emeritus, *Civil*

J.R. Dickinson, professor emeritus, *Electrical*

S.M. Dickinson, professor emeritus, *Mechanical*

G.S. Emmerson, professor emeritus, *Mechanical / History of Medicine & Science*

J.E.K. Foreman, professor emeritus, *Mechanical*

G.A. Geach, professor emeritus, *Materials Science*

N. Kosaric, professor emeritus, *Chemical and Biochemical*

K.Y. Lo, professor emeritus, *Civil*

E.S. Nowak, professor emeritus, *Mechanical*

A.T. Olson, professor emeritus, *Mechanical*

W.H. Peacock, professor emeritus, *Civil*

M.P. Poucher, professor emeritus, *Civil*

K.A. Shelstad, professor emeritus, *Chem & Biochem*

J.W. Stewart, professor emeritus, *Mechanical*

B.J. Vickery, professor emeritus, *Civil*

Appendix 6:
Undergraduate Gold Medal Awards

University Gold Medals

1958	Ross L. Judd	1960	Keith Cross
1959	Gerald K. Vanslyke	1960	Donald Lecocq

Association of Professional Engineers of Ontario (APEO) Gold Medals

1961	G.S. Peter Castle	1976	Robert Bruce McKay
1962	George Bailey	1977	Chi Wah Liu
1963	Allan L. Van Koughnett	1978	John A. Jeffs
1964	Juri Kortschinski	1979	Paul G. Harris
1965	John Ross Grace	1980	John G. Logan
1966	Hugh William Parish	1981	David Paddock
1967	John Christopher Kempling	1982	Kin Man Amazon Lee
1967	Frederick G. Dilkes	1983	Francis Zok
1969	David Robert Brown	1984	Howard M. Heys
1970	Belford Everett Voegelin	1985	Douglas Gordon Roberts
1971	Thomas Fred Dann	1986	Joseph Yee Tak Ng
1972	William Ward Burling	1987	K. Joanne Knight
1973	James Allen Rutledge	1987	R. Bruce Wallace
1974	Shing Shang Lai	1988	Terence Allan Wilson
1975	William Charles Rutledge	1989	Jeffrey Charles Millman

1990	Ian Duncan Reid	2002	Laura Reid
1991	Brian J. Bachmeier	2003	Jeffery Wood
1992	Grace Chung Hang Tong	2004	Lee Betchen
1993	Pamela Ann Marie Renton	2005	Benjamin Fine
1994	Lisa Michelle Becker	2006	Christopher Ward
1995	Douglas Roberts	2007	Anuroop Singh Duggal
1996	Geoffrey Hodgson	2008	Pencilla Lang
1997	Hao Lai	2009	Gregory Kish
1998	Jonathen Michael Southen	2010	Michelle Hennessy
1999	Mikael S. Maki	2011	Jonathan Mcleod
1999	Ian A. Dawes	2012	Kyle Peter Van Hoof
2000	Samir Shergill	2013	Ryan Mitchell Fox
2001	Christopher Scollard		

Appendix 7:
Undergraduate Silver and Gold Medal Awards By Discipline

Chemical

Silver Medal

1961	Michael McKim
1965	John Ross Grace
1967	John Christopher Kempling
1968	Leo Augustus Jr. Behie
1969	Robert Bruce Kok
1970	Belford Everett Voegelin
1971	Peter John Savage
1972	Robert John Henderson
1973	Nicholas Ricciuto
1974	Mario Salvator Buragina
1976	Tze Chuen Kwok
1977	Douglas Walter Muzyka
1978	John Alan Jeffs
1980	Kathryn Jo Anne Harrison
1981	David Paddock
1982	John Blair Wallace
1983	John Alexander Stephenson
1984	Stephen Paul Roberts

1985	Kazimierz Bogdan Jana
1986	Trevor Tsz Leung Ip
1987	K. Joanne Knight

Gold Medal

1988	Thuy Tuong Pham
1989	John Christopher Lynch
1990	Joseph Andrew Richard
1991	Laura Lynn Schinkel
1992	Cheryl Lynn Hudson
1994	Norman Anthony Mensour
1995	Rob Brunet
1996	Michelle Laplante
1997	David A. Files
1998	Gerard Andre Joseph
1999	John M. Murison
2000	Chrysoula Tzaras
2001	Eraclis Tzaras
2002	Jeremy McIntyre
2003	Jeffery Wood

2004	Mustafa Al Sabawi	2009	Federico Berruti
2005	Benjamin Fine	2010	Mark Szynkaruk
2006	Kelly Sedor	2011	Kylie O'Donnell
2007	Sarah Ashleigh Creber	2012	Ryan Waelz
2008	Jie Yu	2013	Kevin Xiangyu Zhou

Civil

Silver Medal

1962	John McCorquodale	1991	Brian Breukelman
1965	Robert E. McPhail	1992	Richard Paul Walker
1966	Richard C. Butler	1993	Richard William I. Brachman
1967	Larry M. Jeffery	1994	Sohrab Movahedi
1970	Marjorie Eleanor Hare	1995	Jon Galsworthy
1971	Robert Alexander Dempsey	1996	Roger Miltenburg
1972	Steven Killing	1997	Brian C. Vanbussel
1973	Peter King	1998	Jonathon Michael Southen
1974	Roy Lai	1999	Mark D'Andrea
1975	Edwin Paul Bryan-Pulham	1999	K. Tory Millar
1977	Stephen Daniel Brown	2000	Corinne Wilmink
1978	Norman Eaarle Hooper	2001	Christopher Scollard
1979	Robert Man Chiu Ng	2002	Laura Reid
1980	David William McKerlie	2003	Jonathon Sumner
1981	Linda Dentay Jollimore	2004	Terri McDermid
1982	Eric MacLeod Holm	2005	Brent Visscher
1984	Elizabeth Anne Brennan	2006	David Gatey
1985	Diana R. Inculet	2007	Winnie Wing-Yin Chan
1986	Joseph Yee Tak Ng	2008	Lisa Katherine Reipas
1987	Ian T. Suttie	2009	Ronald French

Gold Medal

		2010	Michelle Hennessy
		2011	Curtis Williams
1988	Andrew Alexander Fediw	2012	Jonathan Chan
1989	Gregory John Crooks	2013	Yawei Ivy Zhang
1990	Marcus Blaik Kirby		

Computer

Gold Medal
2001 Adam Chaudhary
2001 John Edward
2002 Vivek Singh
2003 Kevin Forbes
2004 Michael Wood
2005 Taha Amiralli

2006 Peter Belej
2007 Bryan Godbolt
2008 Bessam Mustafa
2009 Polad Zahedi
2010 Curtis Conway
2011 Amar Zebian
2012 Kyle Degannes

Electrical

Silver Medal
1961 G.S. Peter Castle
1962 Arthur Marriage
1963 Robert Russell Marley
1964 Leonard George Stass
1965 Gordon Sherlock Aitken
1966 Hugh William Parish
1967 Murray Edward Coultes
1968 William D. Greason
1969 Borys Koba
1970 Kok Pan Tang
1971 Matthew Albert Bol
1972 William Ward Burling
1973 Ronald William Evans
1974 Alan Francis Hawtin
1975 Norman Joseph Slater
1976 Robert Bruce McKay
1977 Hon Fay Yu
1978 George Maynard Hart
1979 Wang-Leung Ignatius Lan
1980 John Garfield Logan
1981 Bernard Juneau

1982 James Howard McClelland
1983 John Russell McMacken
1984 Robert Gordon Lankin
1985 Douglas Gordon Roberts
1986 Chi Tak Tong
1987 Raymond Bruce Wallace

Gold Medal
1988 Terence Allan Wilson
1989 Arnold Veenstra
1991 Frank Wayne Singor
1992 Grace Chung Hang Tong
1993 Michael James Simpson
1994 Ka Fai Ng
1995 Claude Gauthier
1996 David A.D. Tompkins
1997 Hao Lai
1998 Kevin Michael Kuntz
1999 Ian A. Dawes
2000 Edward Doe
2001 Vanja Subotic
2002 Brian Patenaude
2003 Lee Rehorn

2004	Chirag Patel	2009	Gregory Kish
2005	David Suelzle	2010	Mark Neumann
2006	Nima Rohani	2011	Jonathan Mcleod
2007	Anuroop Singh Duggal	2012	Kyle Peter Van Hoof
2008	Malgorzata Markowski	2013	Ryan Mitchell Fox

Green Process

Gold Medal

2012	Thomas Butler	2013	Harrison Ward

Integrated

Gold Medal

2002	Matthew Pickard	2008	Al-Karim Moloo
2003	Nicholas Jankovic	2009	Stephanie Puzio
2005	Thomas Ewart	2010	Brian Putre
2007	Lorcan Anthony Kilmartin	2011	Shane Parkhill
		2012	Vincey Man Kwan Chui

Materials

Silver Medal

1972	Arthur Alexander Hornibrook
1975	Manfred Kling
1977	Robert Bryant
1981	Calvin T. Kaltenback
1983	Francis Zok
1985	John David Wice
1986	Edward Mark Lehockey

Gold Medal

1987	Warren J. Poole
1989	Kathryn Julia O'Hagan
1991	Doris Bernadette Sabljic
1993	A.H. Hilary Clarke
1995	A. Jason Hendry
1997	Christopher J. Rolls
1998	Caroline Andrewes
2000	Lori-Anne Williams
2001	Jessica Wolfe

Mechanical

Silver Medal

1962	Gorge Raithby
1964	Gerald W.T. Trick
1965	Terrence S. Robinson
1966	Jack W. Warren
1967	Ronald H. Schill
1968	Frederick G. Dilkes
1969	David Robert Brown
1970	Philip William Jones
1971	Thomas Fred Dann
1973	James Allen Rutledge
1974	Donald Andress Bayly
1975	William Charles Rutledge
1976	Garry Leonard Jon Rustan
1977	Chi Wah Liu
1978	Steven David Hartman
1979	Paul Glendon Harris
1980	Keith Wallace
1981	Edward Kwok Hay Liu
1982	Brian Harschnitz
1983	David Naylor
1984	Siew Kiat Chua
1985	Gordon John Phillips
1986	Jonathan William MacDonald
1987	David M. Pascoe

Gold Medal

1988	Wayne Kevin Hutchison
1989	Jeffrey Charles Millman
1990	J. Julian Mills-Cockell
1991	Brian J. Bachmeier
1992	Stephanie Ruth Wilkes
1993	John Nji Chi
1994	Lisa Michelle Becker
1995	Douglas Roberts
1996	Geoffrey R. Hodgson
1997	Kent Sinmaz
1998	Jeffrey Bruce DeRooy
1999	Mikael S. Maki
2000	Jeremy Sluyters
2001	Trevor Davis
2002	Nathan Hazzard
2003	Philip Metcalf
2004	Lee Betchen
2005	Greg Wolfe
2006	Christopher Ward
2007	John Ghazal
2008	David Cesar Del Rey Fernandez
2009	Brian Coulter
2010	Kevin Elliott
2011	Rachel Brown
2012	Jacob Reeves
2013	Aaron Yurkewich

Software

Gold Medal

2001	John Edward	2007	David Allison
2002	Aaron Coady	2008	Rizwan Teipar
2003	Rebecca McKillican	2009	Joshua Bart
2004	Brent Hands	2010	Kevin Brown
2005	Siddharth Datta	2011	Adam Van Ymeren
2006	Keith Holman	2012	Bishoy Joseph Ghobrial
		2013	Steven Jason Walt

Appendix 8:
L. S. Lauchland Engineering Alumni Medals

The L.S. Lauchland Engineering Alumni Medal was initiated in 1976 to mark the retirement of Professor L. Stuart Lauchland, past president of APEO.

- 1977 Dr. Ross Leonard Judd, BESc'58
- 1979 Dr. Michael Owen Toll, BESc'68
- 1981 Mr. Carl Erik Kohn, BESc'64
- 1982 Mr. Steven Killing, BESc'72
- 1984 Dr. John R. Grace, BESc'65
- 1986 Mr. Peter C. Maurice, BESc'60
- 1989 Mr. John M. Thompson, O.C.,BESc'66
- 1990 Mr. Brian Hewat, BESc'59
- 1991 Mr. Ron Yamada, BESc'64
- 1994 Mr. Bill Etherington, BESc'63
- 1997 Mr. Jack McBain, BESc'66
- 1998 Mr. Henry Yip, BESc'73
- 1999 Mr. John Westeinde, BESc'62
- 2001 Mr. John Jardine, BESc'65
- 2002 Mr. Douglas Muzyka, BESc'77, MESc.'78, PhD'85
- 2003 Mr. Ted Aziz, BESc'60
- 2004 Dr. G.S. Peter Castle, BESc'61, PhD'69
- 2005 Mr. Keith Zerebecki, BESc'72, MEng.'73
- 2006 Mr. Charles Ruigrok, BESc'78, MESc'84

- 2007 Mr. Boris Jackman, BESc'72
- 2008 Ms. Catherine Karakatsanis, BESc'83, MESc'91
- 2009 Ms. Sarah Shortreed, BESc'89
- 2011 Keith Stevens, BESc'70, MESc'71
- 2012 James Douglas (J.D.) Hole, BESc'67
- 2013 Hanny A. Hassan, C.M., BESc'64

Appendix 9:
Advisory Council for Western Engineering (ACWE) Chairs

The Faculty of Engineering at Western University is pleased to recognize the following ACWE chairs for their volunteer commitment to the faculty:

1954 – 1964	Edward Victor Buchanan
1965	D.B. Strudley
1966 – 1970	K.F. Tupper
1971 – 1972	J.B. Cronyn
1973	Duncan Donald C. McGeachy
1974	G.E. Wilson
1975 – 1976	George W. Chorley
1977	C.S. Lare
1978 – 1980	Vacant
1981	Edward Michael Aziz
1982	James Miller Hay
1983	Carl Erik Kohn
1984	J. Warren
1985 – 1986	David John Naish
1987	John Munro Thompson
1988	Walter Petryschuk
1989 – 1990	Ronald H. Yamada
1991 – 1992	Peter Charles Maurice

1993 – 1994	William Albert Etherington
1995	David J. Smith
1998 – 1999	Allan George Bulckaert
1999 – 2001	Marvi Ricker (Acting Chair)
2001 – 2006	Ginny Dybenko
2006 – 2010	James Serack
2011 –	Catherine Karakatsanis

Appendix 10:
Faculty Administrators

Deans

1960 – 1970	Dr. Richard M. Dillon
1971 – 1977	Dr. A.I. Johnson
1978 – 1987	Dr. Gordon F. Chess
1987 – 1999	Dr. R. Mohan Mathur
2000 – 2007	Dr. Franco Berruti
2008 – 2009	Dr. George Knopf (Acting Dean)
2009 –	Dr. Andrew Hrymak

Associate Deans

Academic

1971 – 1975	Dr. G.S. Peter Castle
1975 – 1978	Dr. Gordon F. Chess
1984 – 1987	Dr. William D. Davis
1987 – 1993	Dr. Ian J. Duerden
1993 – 1996	Dr. Tom Bonnema
1996 – 2001	Dr. J. Maciej Floryan
2001 – 2003	Dr. Raouf Baddour
2003 – 2007	Dr. George Knopf
2008 – 2012	Dr. Amarjeet Bassi
2013 –	Dr. Michael Bartlett

Research/Graduate

2004 –	Dr. Hesham El Naggar
2001 – 2004	Dr. Cedric Briens
1997 – 2001	Dr. Ian D. Moore
1989 – 1997	Dr. Jan M. Beeckmans
1988 – 1989	Dr. R. Kerry Rowe
1971 – 1975	Dr. Jim Zajic

Chairs

Core Studies

G.S. Emmerson	1967 – 1973
R.K. Swartman	1973 – 1976
J.D. Tarasuk	1976 – 1979
T. Bonnema	1979 – 1985

Chemical (and Biochemical)

J. L. Kearns	1960 – 1965
W. Bulani	1965 – 1971
J.E. Zajic	1971 – 1973
M.A. Bergougnou	1973 – 1975
J.M. Beeckmans	1975 – 1978
	1984 – 1989
N. Kosaric	1978 – 1981
K.A. Shelstad	1981 – 1984
A. Margaritis	1989 – 1999
S. Rohani	1999 – 2009
A. Ray	2009 –

Civil

M.P. Poucher	1960 – 1973
	1978 – 1992

A.G. Davenport   1973 – 1978
R.K. Rowe   1992 – 2000
I. Moore   2000
R. Baddour   2001 – 2001
E. Yanful   2001 – 2012
A. El Damatty   2012 –

Electrical

L.S. Lauchland   1960 – 1970
I.I. Inculet   1970 – 1976
G.F. Chess   1976 – 1979
G.S.P. Castle   1979 – 1984
                     1989 – 1994
A.R. Webster   1984 – 1989
                     1994 – 1999
R. V. Patel   1999 – 2003
T. S. Sidhu   2003 – 2011
S. Primak (Acting)   2011 – 2012
K. McIsaac   2013 –

Materials Science

G.A. Geach   1964 – 1969
J.D. Brown   1969 – 1975
                     1988 – 1994
                     1995 – 1996
J.S. Sheasby   1975 – 1983
                     1984 – 1987
                     1996 – 1998
I.J. Duerden   1994 – 1995

Mechanical

J.E.K. Foreman	1960 – 1972
E.S. Nowak	1972 – 1975
A.T. Olson	1975 – 1982
S.M. Dickinson	1982 – 1985
J.D. Tarasuk	1985 – 1999

Mechanical and Materials

J. S. Sheasby	1999 – 2003
R. Martinuzzi	2003 – 2004 (Acting)
J. M. Floryan	2004 –
A. Straatman	2009 – 2011 (Acting)